PRAISE FOR "A BEARDE'S EYE VIEW"

As someone who often gets asked for testimonials and endorsements, as soon as I saw a request from Chris Bearde to say something nice about his new wonderfully hilarious book, I immediately said, "Who?"
Jeffrey Robinson - International author and lecturer. Best known for "The Laundrymen" "Yamani – The Inside Story" "Rainier & Grace" and "The Risk Takers"

When I met Chris in the 70's words meant different things. Hep was becoming hip...crazy meant wonderful...bad was the new good and cool meant hot.

-

So Chris arrived in Tinsel Town as a bad dude...who was hip, and cool and crazy...And oh yes, he was funny which meant the same then that it means now.
George Schlatter - Producer of "Rowan & Martin's Laugh-In"

CHRIS BEARDE, a man who views life as a comedy and has been able to laugh his way through it.
Bob Einstein - Actor, Writer, Producer, Comedian...Super Dave

CHRIS BEARDE...What a guy. When Hollywood beckoned to him (with a solid gold forefinger), it smiled with delight? I was with him when he won a limerick contest on my show by sending in a label from a can of carbonated squid and a torn mask! A great talent – Congrats on your new book. We're so happy you wrote so much of it in Farsi!
Gary Owens – Television and radio icon.

ACKNOWLEGMENTS

Thanks to the East Sydney Technical College art course for my first steps in penmanship.

Thank you to Charlie Chaplin, Jaques Tati, Danny Kaye and Jerry Lewis for my university course in the art of the sight gag.

INTRODUCTION

It was always a fun thing to be able to draw. When I was a teenager growing up in my adopted homeland of Australia being able to express oneself in art was a big plus. In those days' only really smart kids and rich kids could go on to a full four years of college in Sydney. The rest of us peasants had to leave school at 15 and go to work, semi-child labor so to speak.

I was fortunate enough to have a dad in advertising who wrote copy and designed ads for a company called George Paterson's. He arranged for me to get a free commercial art scholarship at the East Sydney Technical College in Darlinghurst. In return I became a runner for the adverting agency during the day and went to college three nights a week from 6 to 9.30 pm. Being a strapping young junior champion surfer at South Narrabeen Surf Club and playing every sport imaginable, it was easy to take the long hours. What wasn't so easy to take was the fact that I didn't feel right with the static quality of painting, lettering, still life etc., although I did enjoy the nude models both for studying and other stuff that art students did with nude models.

There was a weekly movie night that started after class in the library of this great old convict built jail that had been converted to the art school years before. I started attending these showings and soon found that watching Charlie Chaplin, Ben Turpin, Charlie Chester, Buster Keaton and Harold Lloyd got my mojo working better than painting a vase of flowers or a pastoral scene of a sheep farm. You go to college to grow up and find out what you really want to do with your life. It was in that convict built building that I was set free to begin a life in comedy. From those early days on I knew all I really wanted to do was make people laugh. As the years went on I was provided with the ways and means to do just that.

When television first came to Australia we beatnik jazz loving students would gather at a café at Kings Cross called the El Morocco to watch Sunday night television. Viewing all this action contained within in a frame was my answer to what I needed to push me to the next step. It was pretty simple I wanted to make people laugh on television! So I did, both in Australia in the very early days of television where I hosted a three day a week kids show called "Smalltime"...and worked in a 2 hour Saturday Morning kids show called "Captain Fortune's Saturday Party"...and on through writing and performing in Australia's most successful variety series REVUE 61' and 62', and then to Canada under contract to the CBC in Toronto where the laughs continued for 5 years of Canada's most popular late night show "Nightcap".

Hardly stopping to take a breath the laughs kept coming when I moved to Hollywood and they've been coming ever since. One of the most important qualities of this success has always been the ability to illustrate my thoughts and ideas in rough drawings and sketches, and that didn't stop, just like the laughter didn't. So this little book of cartoons was a labor of a comedy writer's second love… the delight in continuing to be able draw for fun. I hope you get a few laughs from "A Bearde's Eye View", and if anything offends you...It was meant to as I am a radical left wing sexist with a chip about almost everything…how I've stayed married to the poor woman who helped me edit and produce this book is beyond belief.
Chris Bearde

A BEARDE'S EYE VIEW

"Cartoons From The Id"

By
Chris Bearde

Published by Stonecloud Publishing

CONTACT INFO:
info@chrisbearde.com
www.chrisbearde.com
310 401.3110

ISBN: 10: 0615564216
ISBN-13: 978 0-615-56421

DEDICATION

This is for my lovely, talented wife and partner, Carolyn

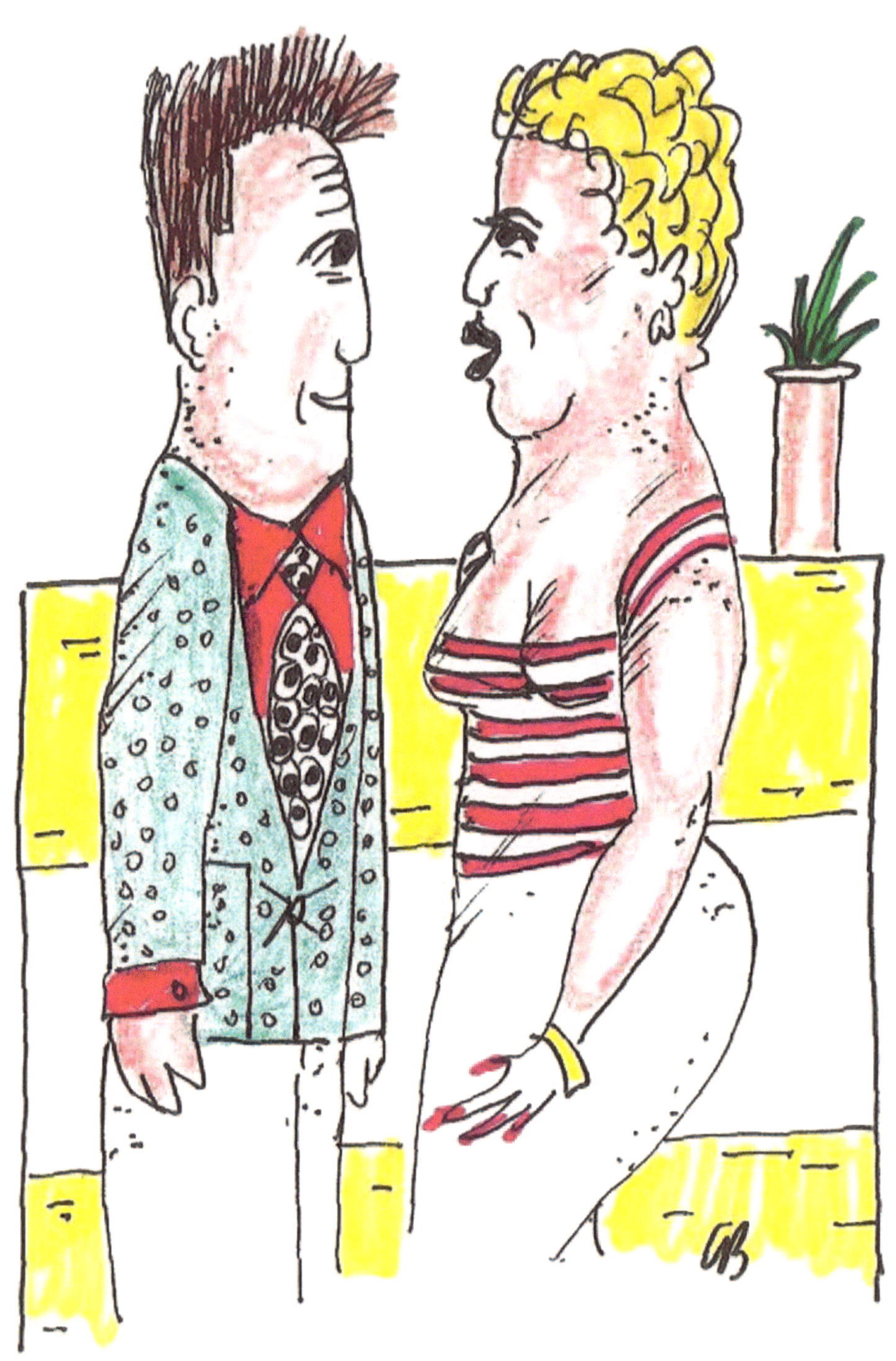

“I didn’t know there was a 6th Beatle!”

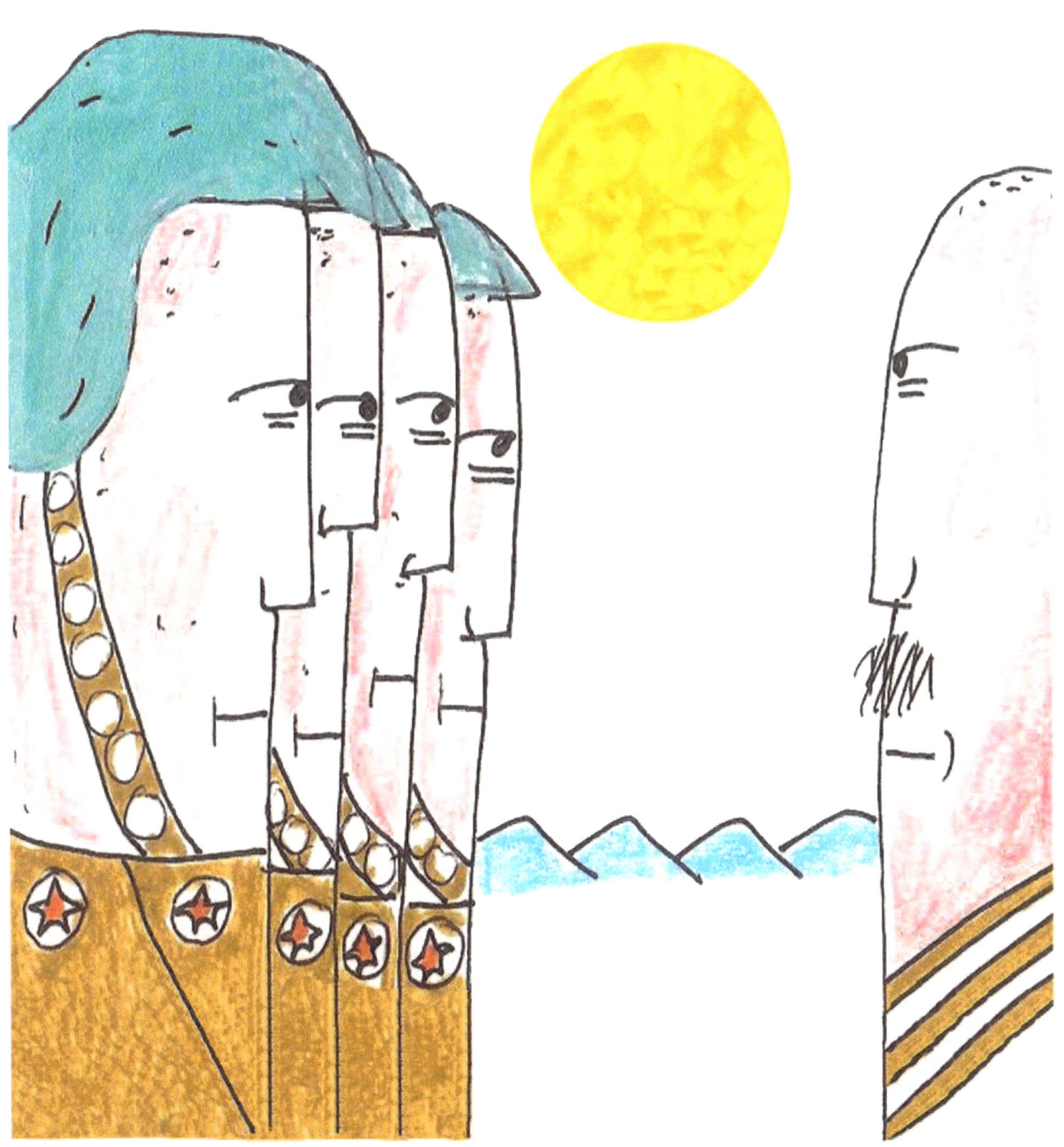

“Which on of you men applied for an audition at Dancing With The Stars?”

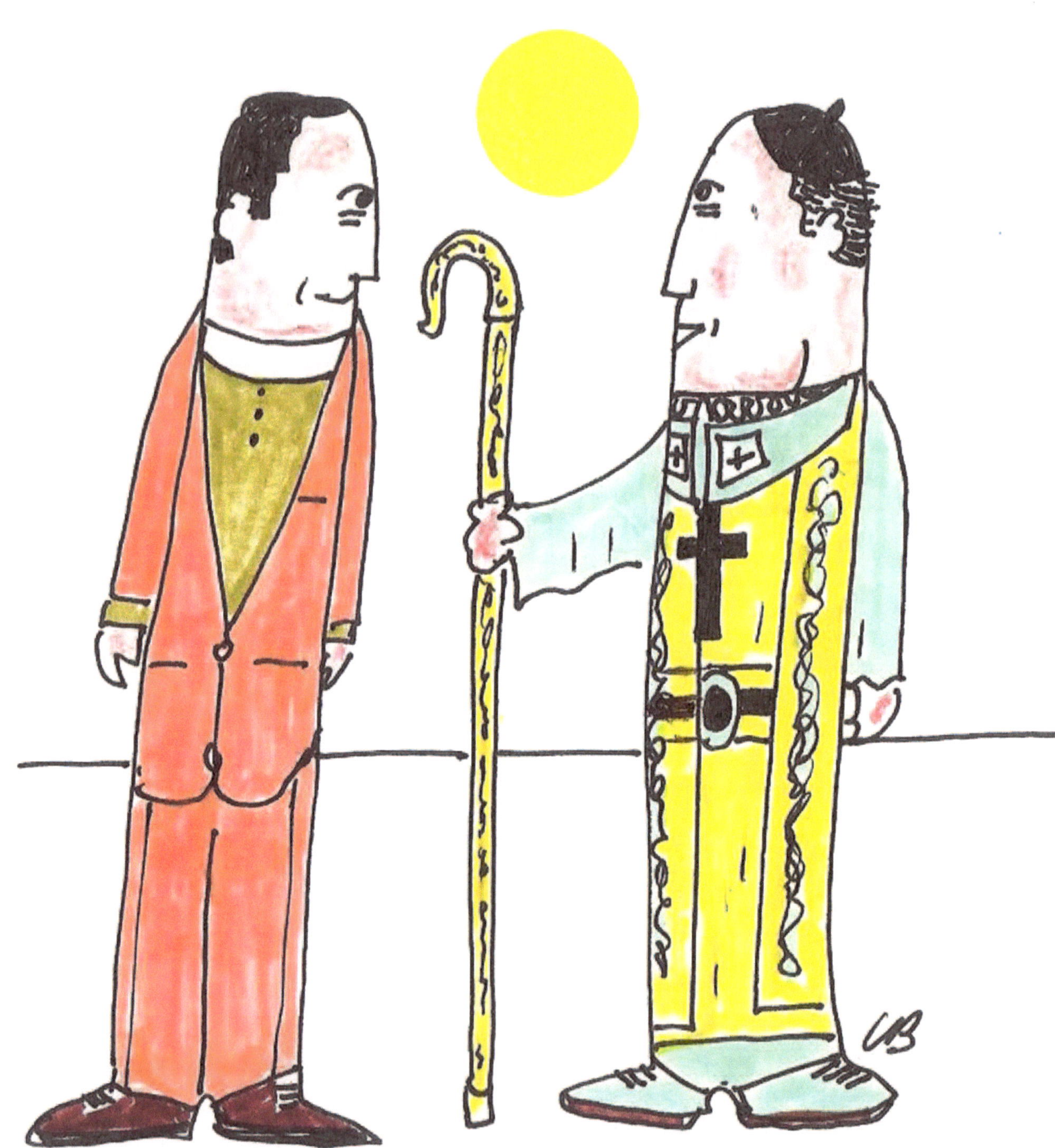

"Some of my best friends are choir boys."

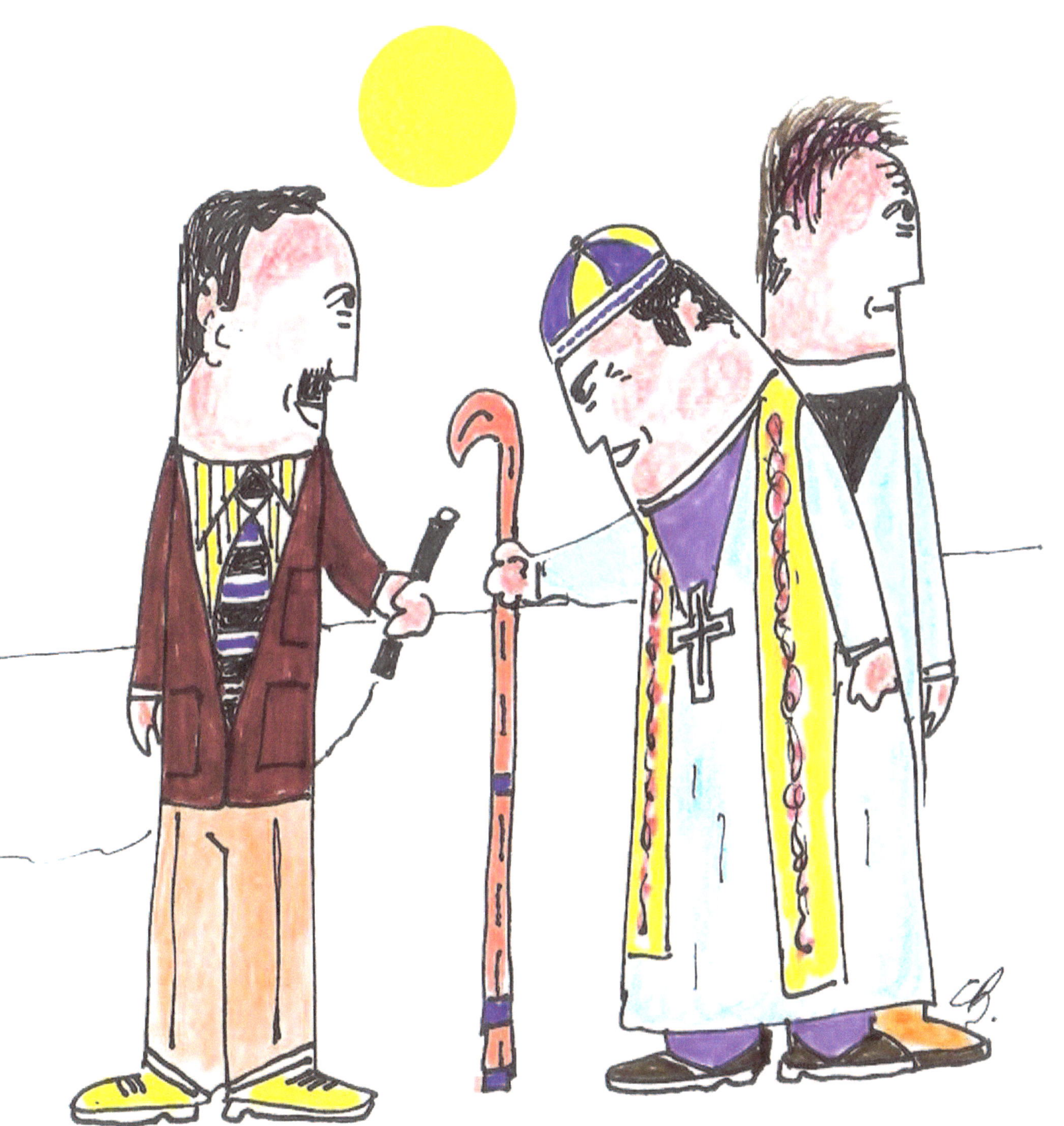

“The menu tonight is Body of Christ & Oysters Rockefeller.”

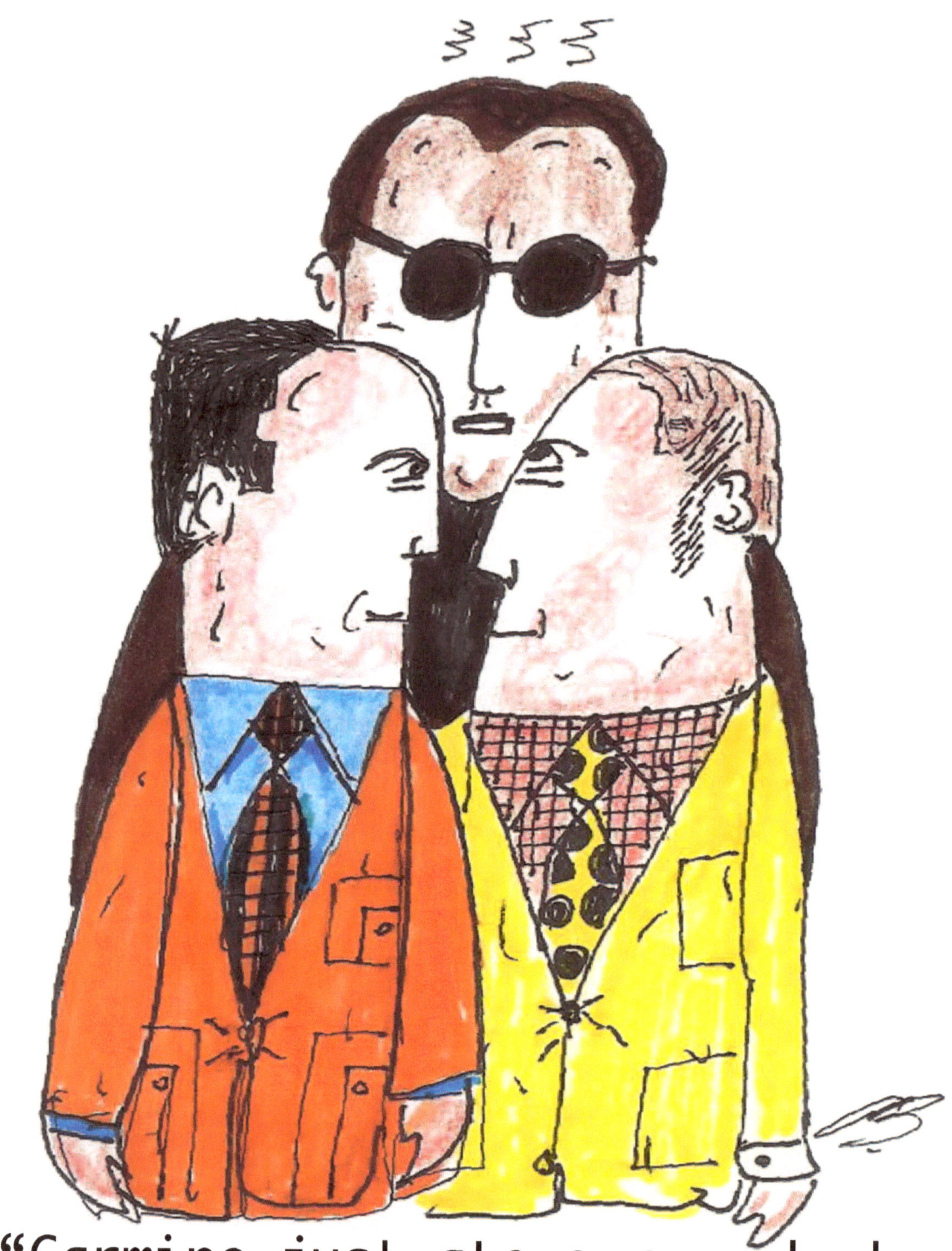

"Carmine just ate our cooked books!"

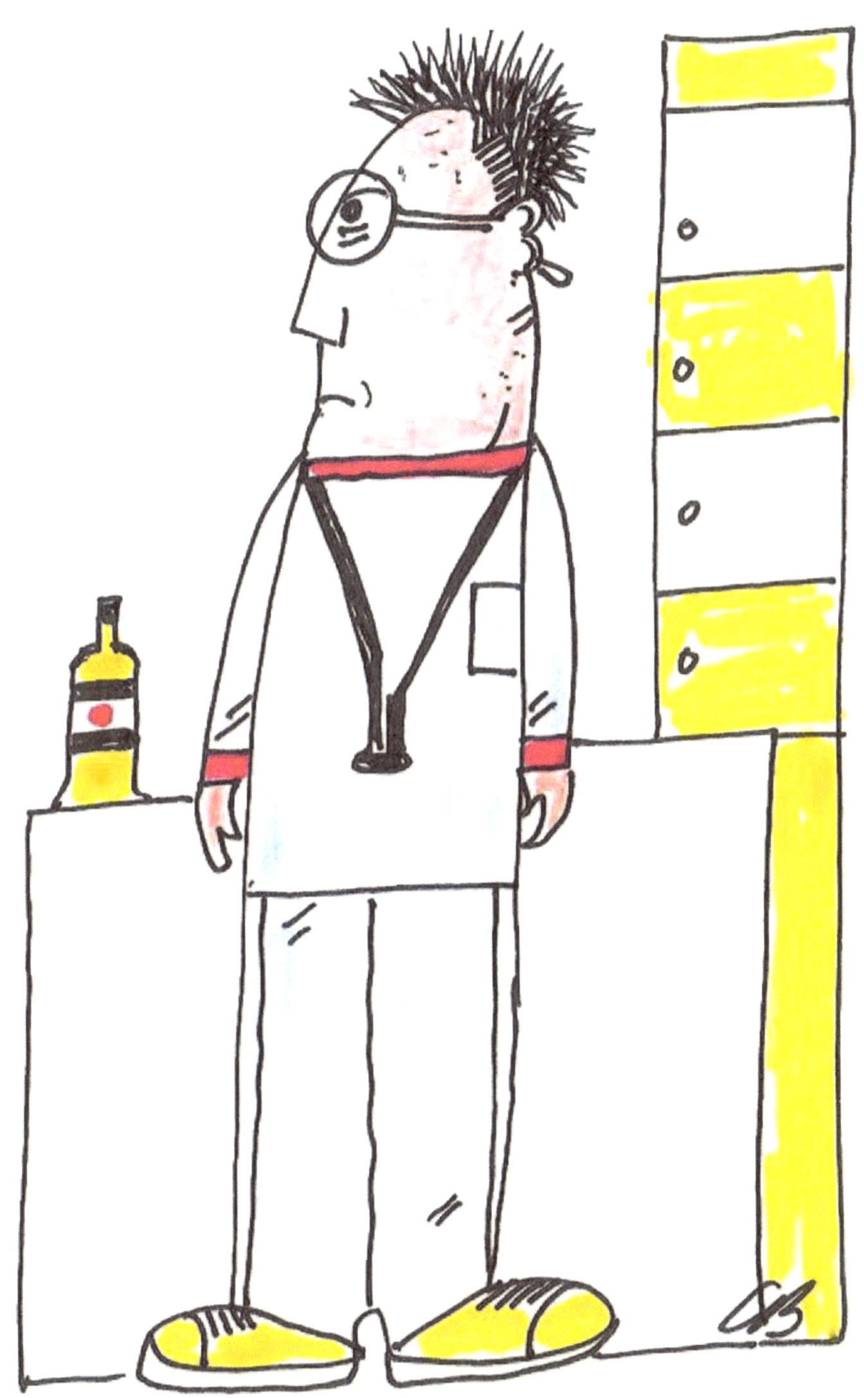

“Doctor I think I’ve cloned the wrong Jonas brother!”

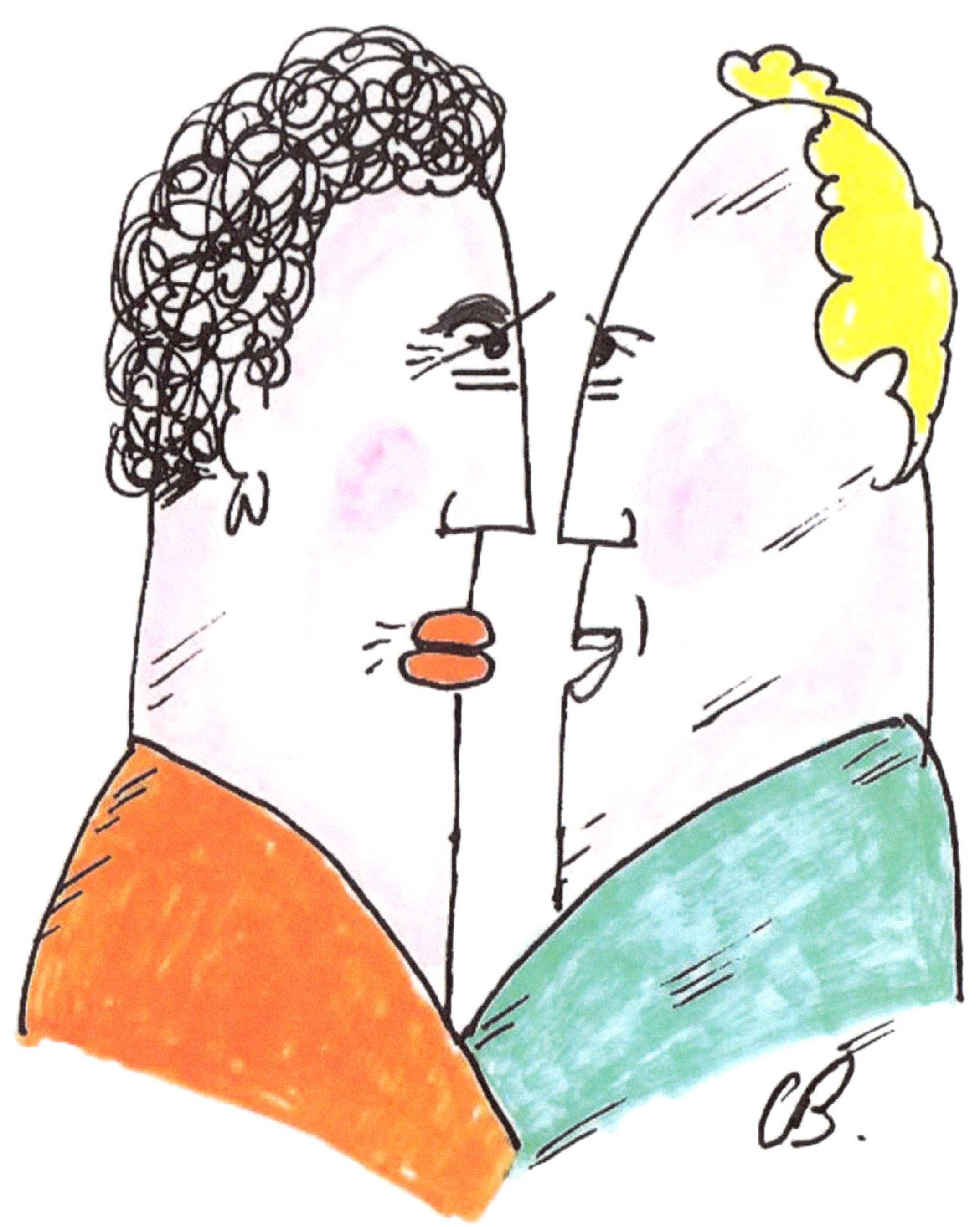

"Your credit card is so over the limit...it melted!"

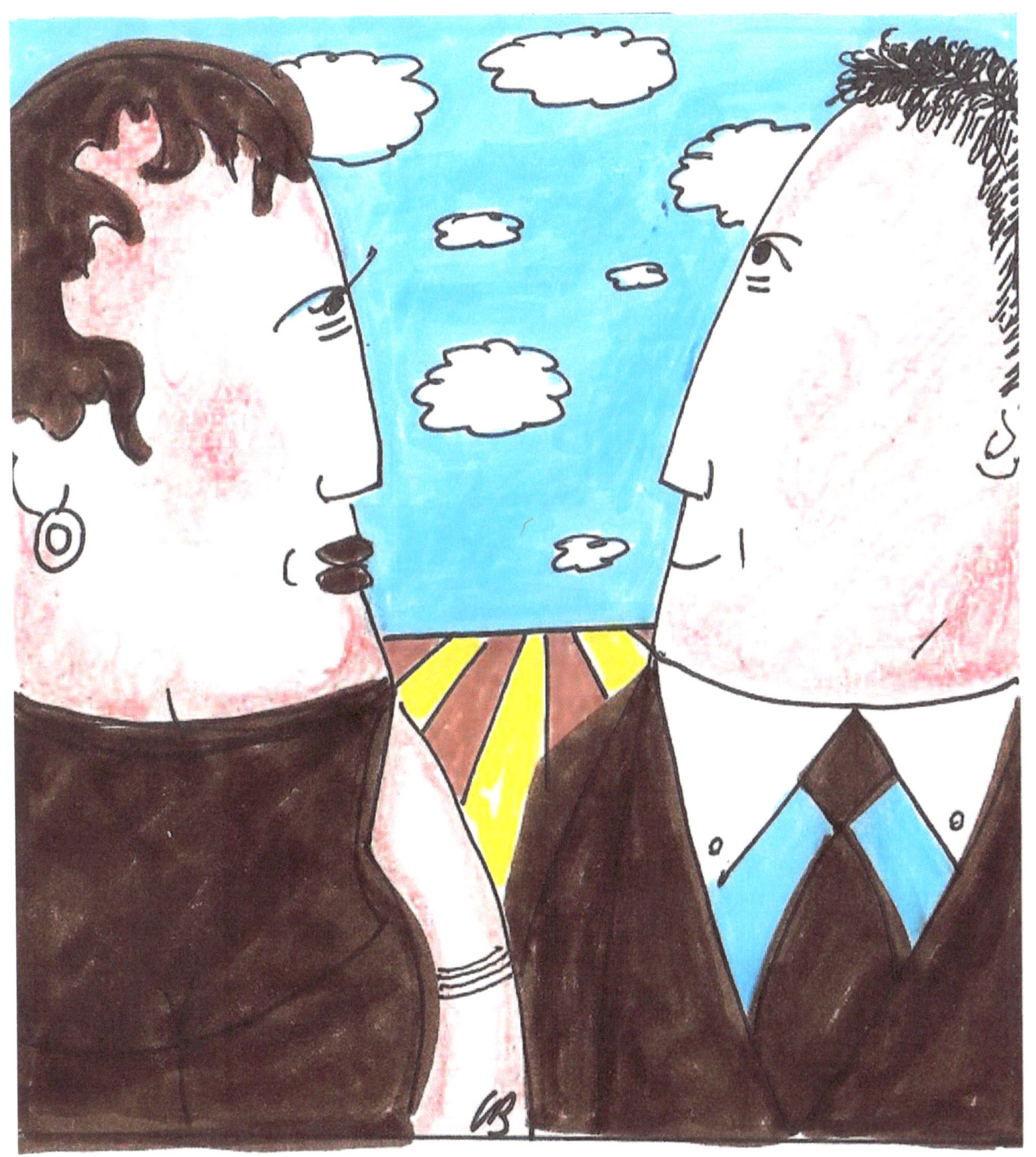

“I’ve reached my Facebook limit. You want a few spare friends?”

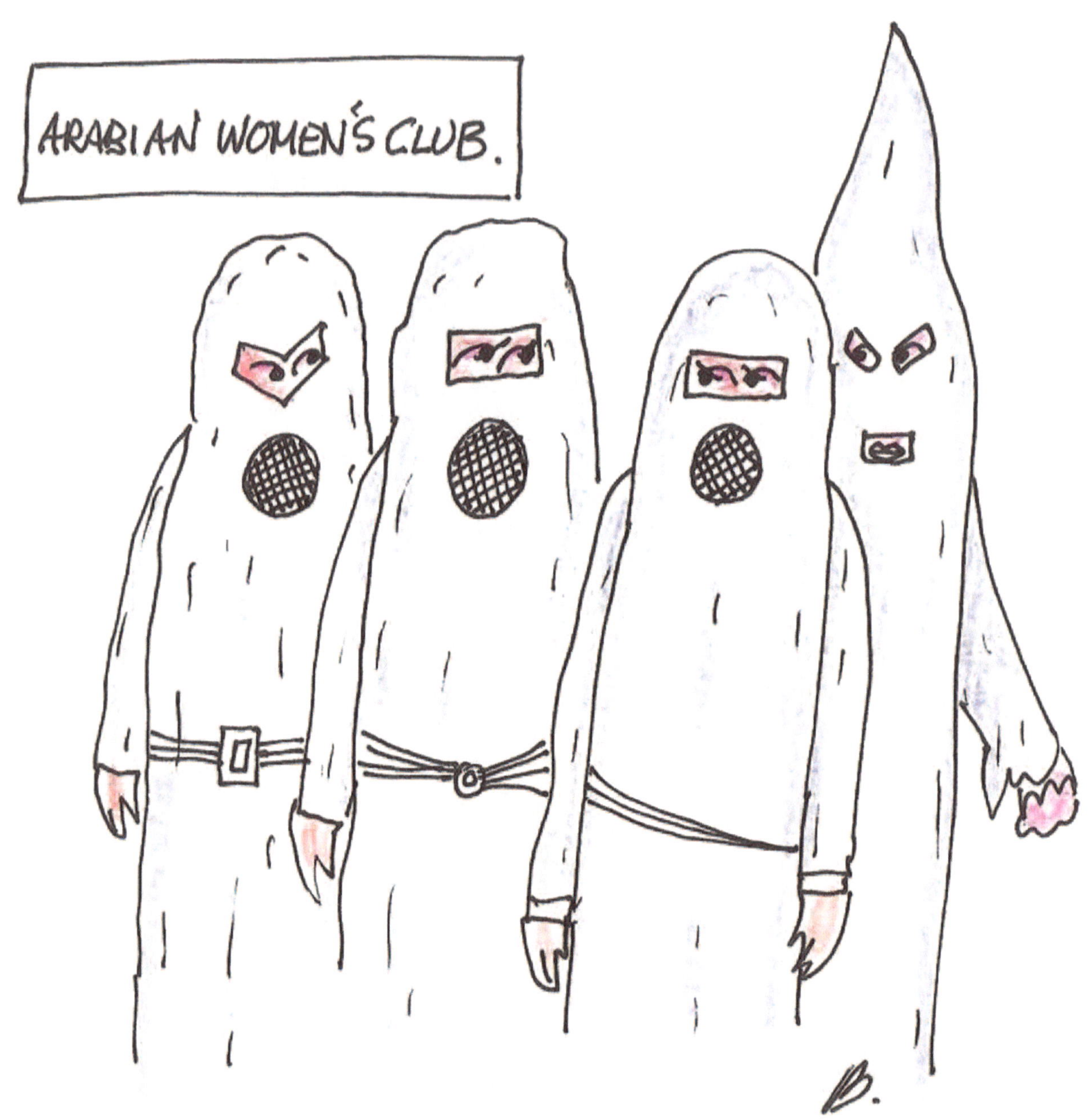

“Who invited the new girl?”

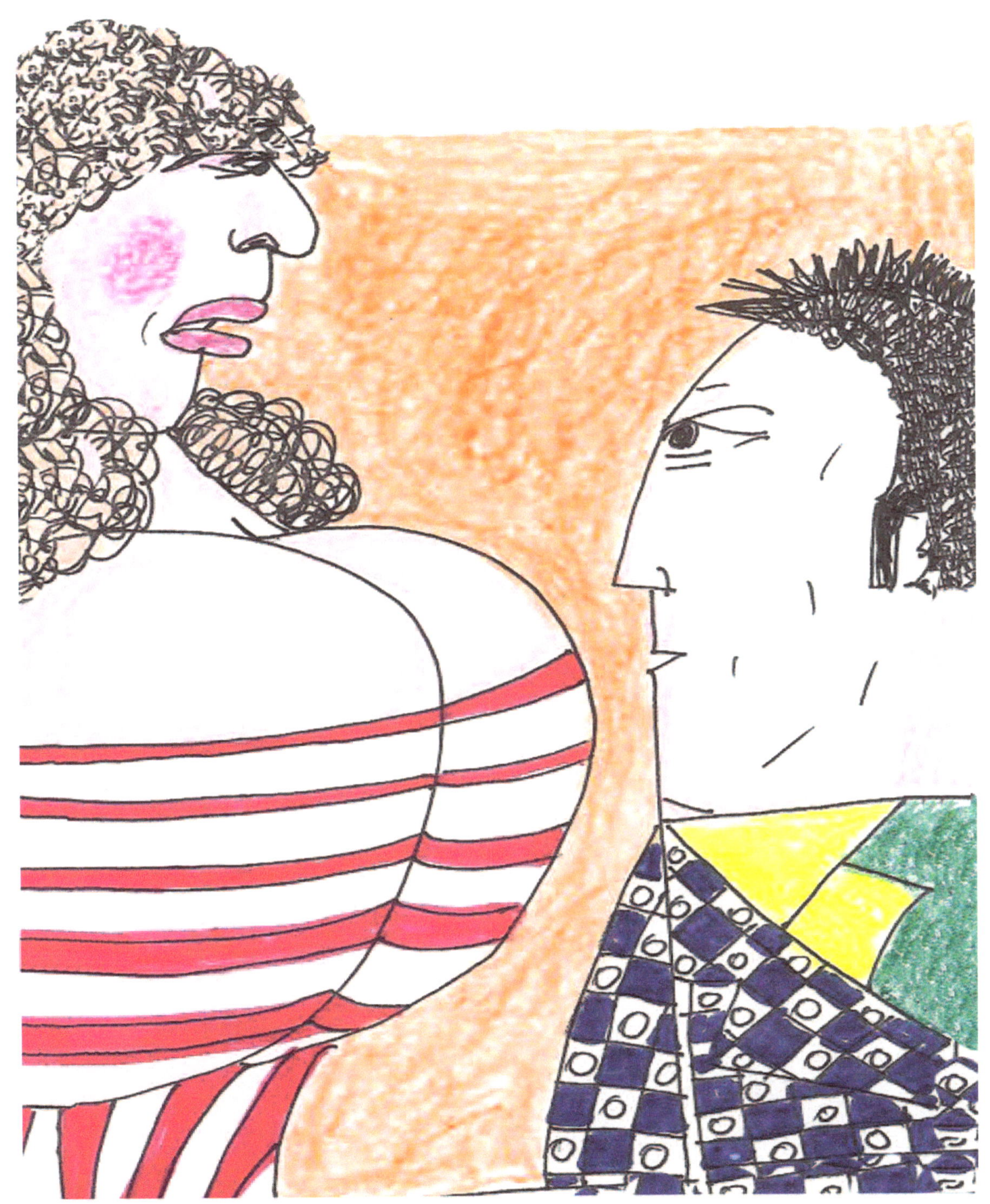

"The historic flight of the Hindenberg comes to mind."

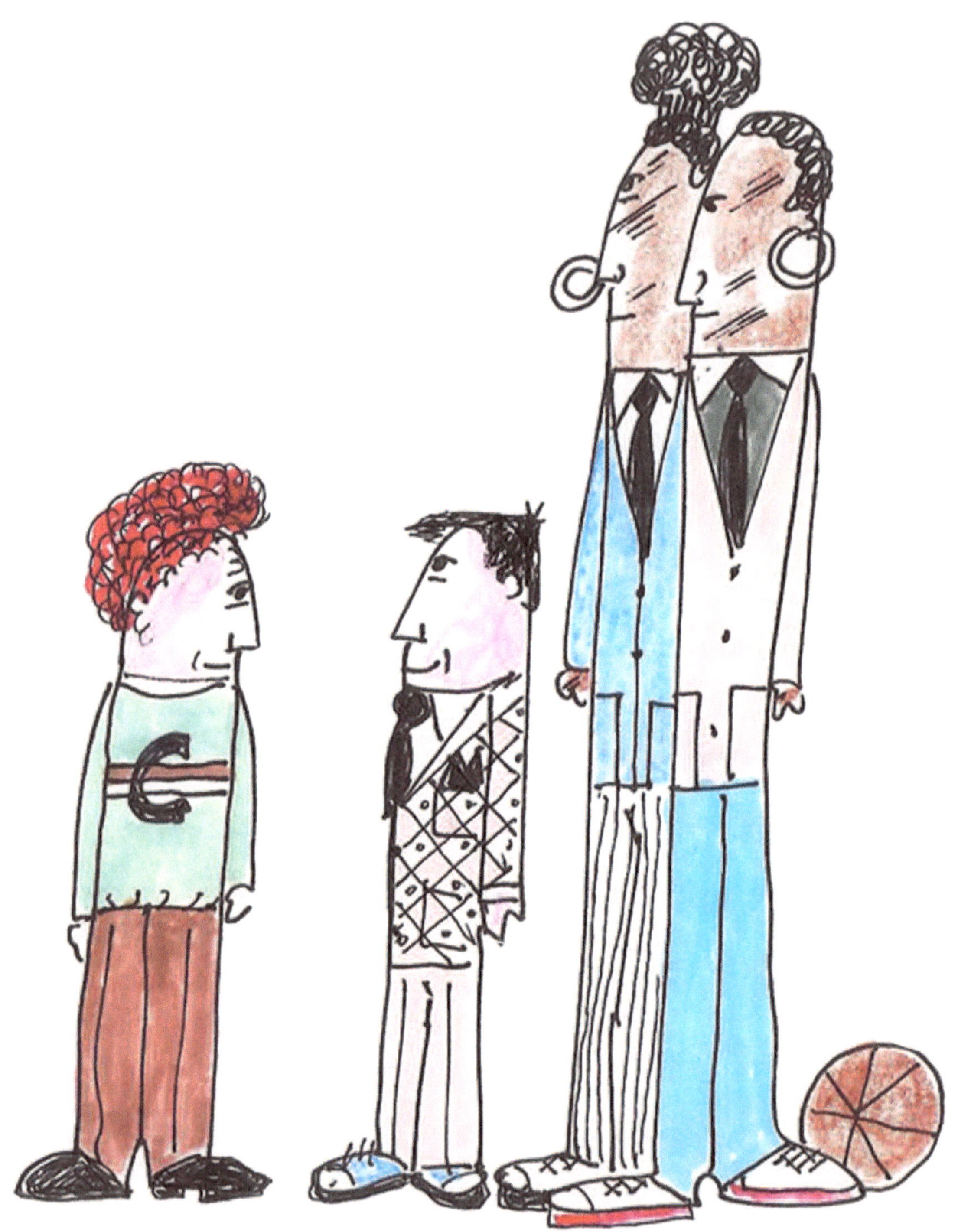

“These are two players from Senegal who will be playing for peanuts and a roof.”

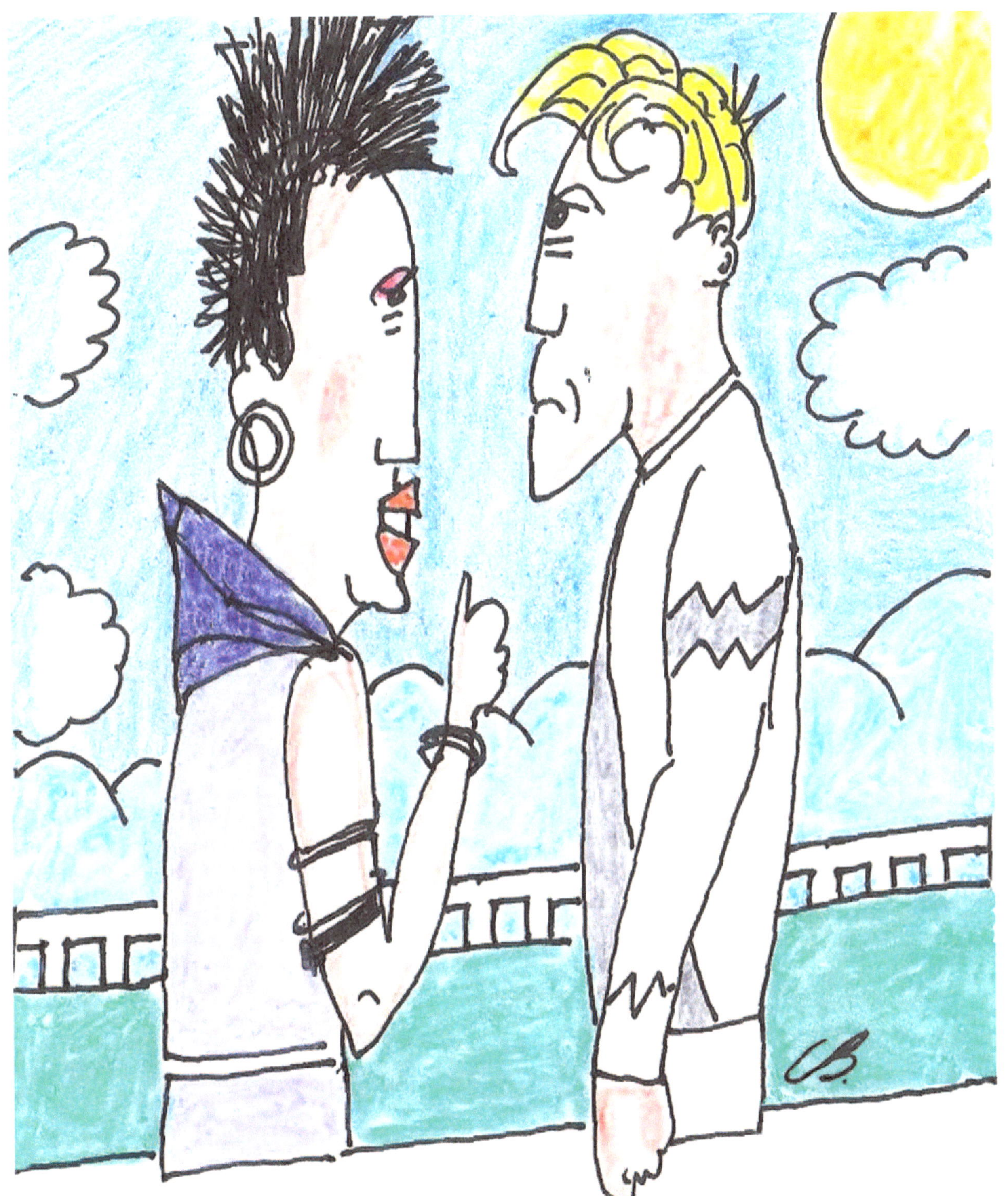

"My husband is out looking for a spine."

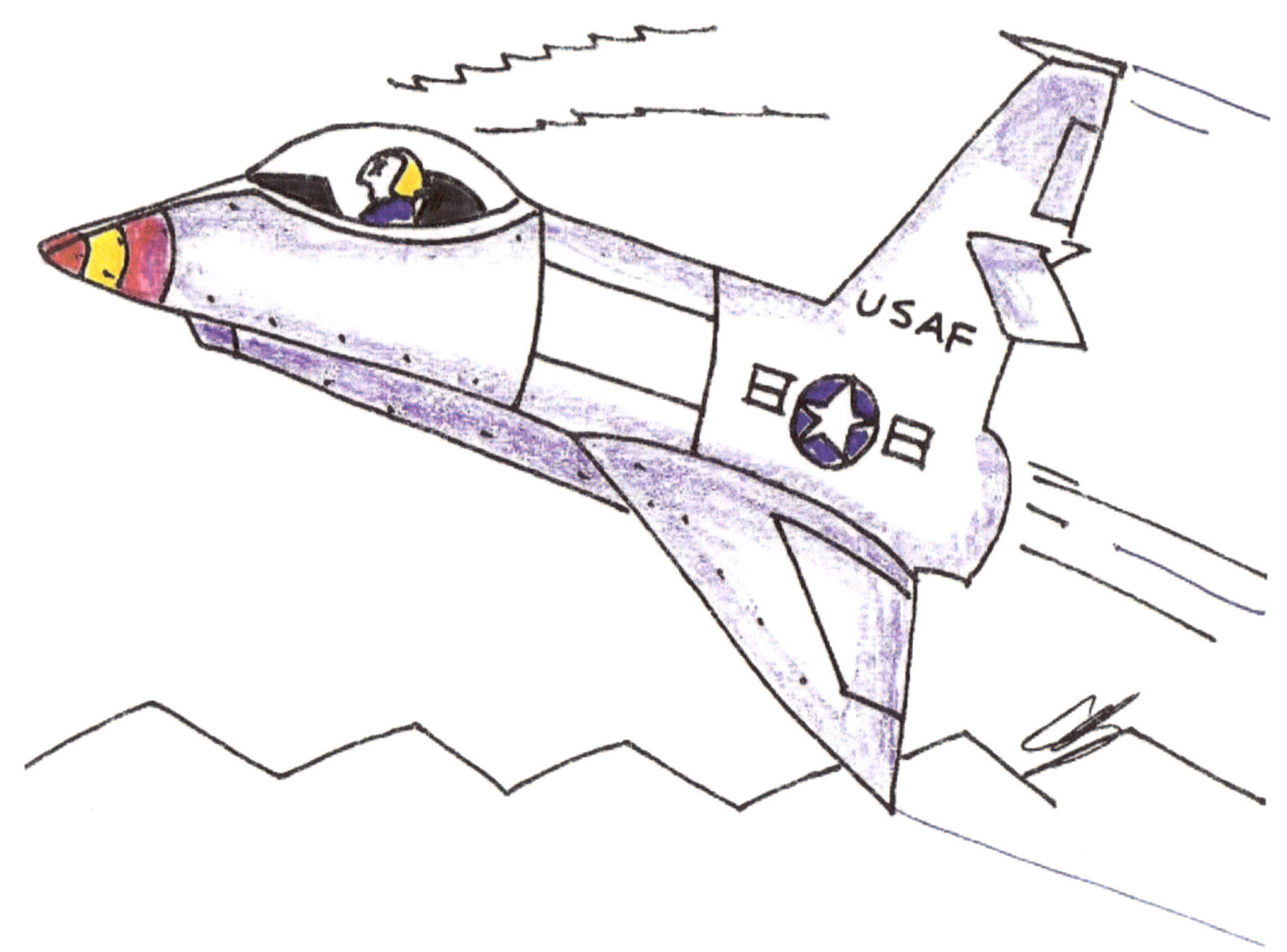

“I think I just bombed an empty cave that I already bombed when it was empty before.”

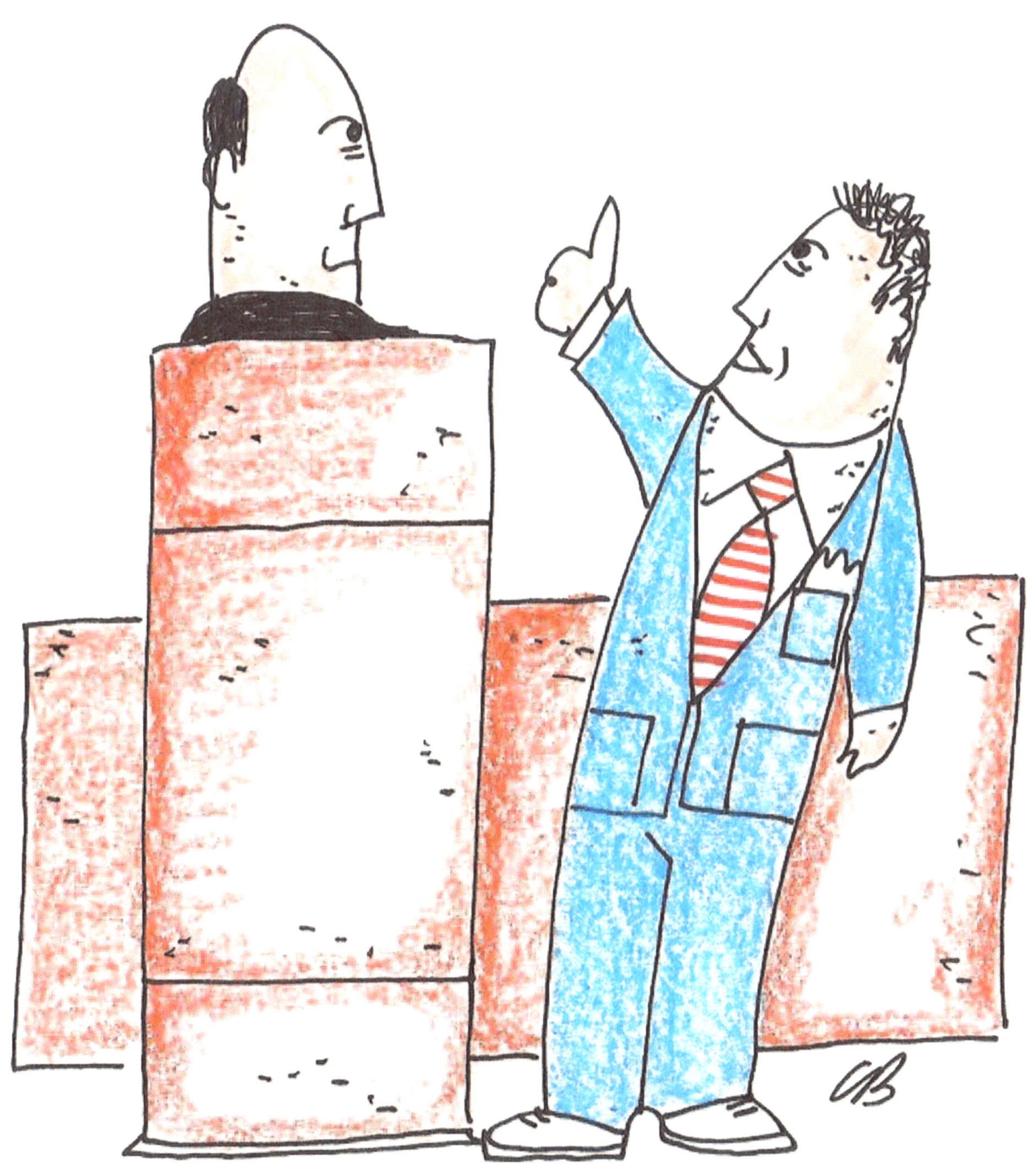

"Your Honor, I demand a retread."

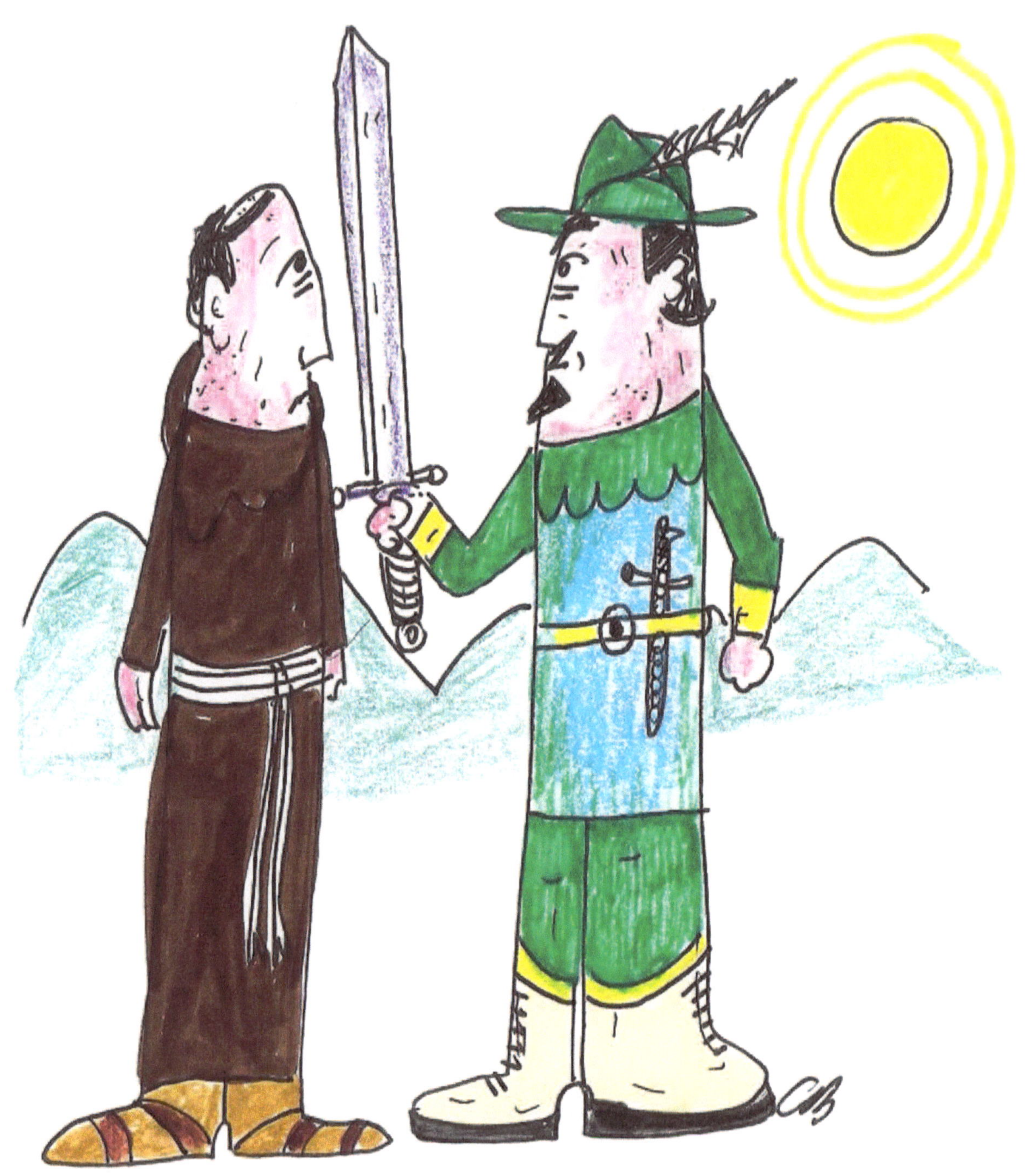

“Tell Friar Tuck, I shot the Sheriff, but I didn’t shoot the deputy.”

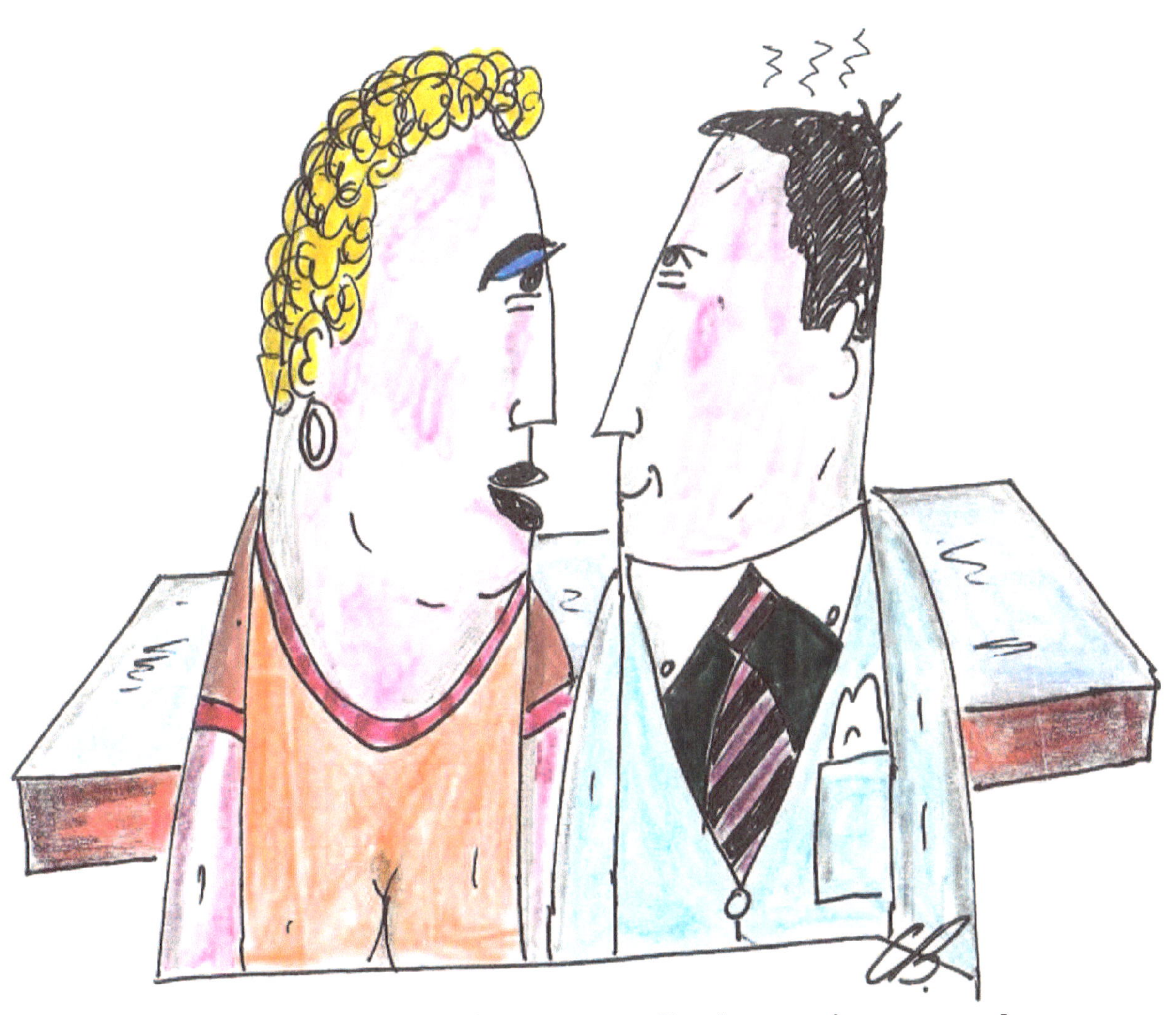

"I'm thinking of having the step-children over for a judgmental lunch."

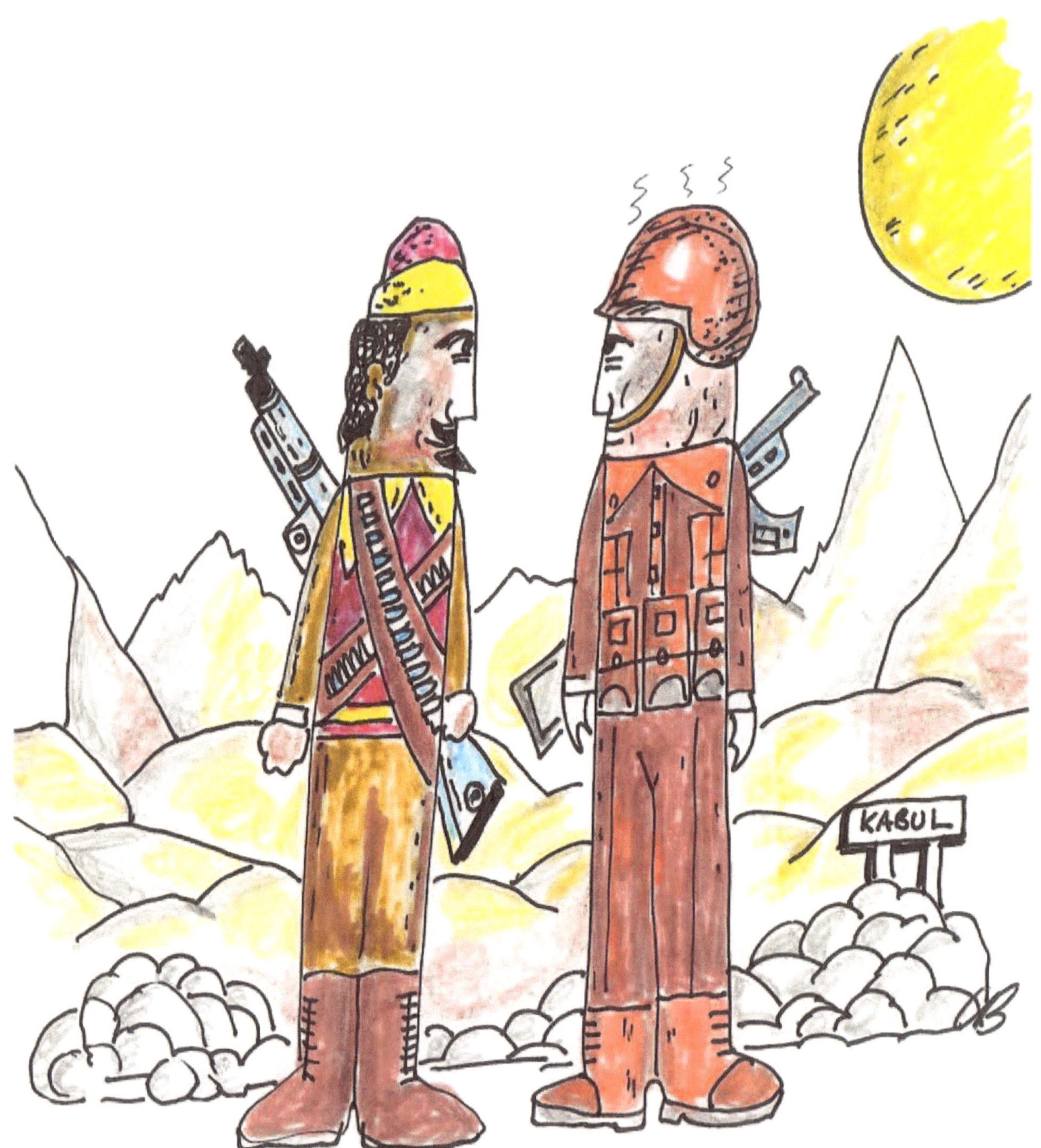

"The Americans have been here for 10 years. Isn't it time for a change of underwear?"

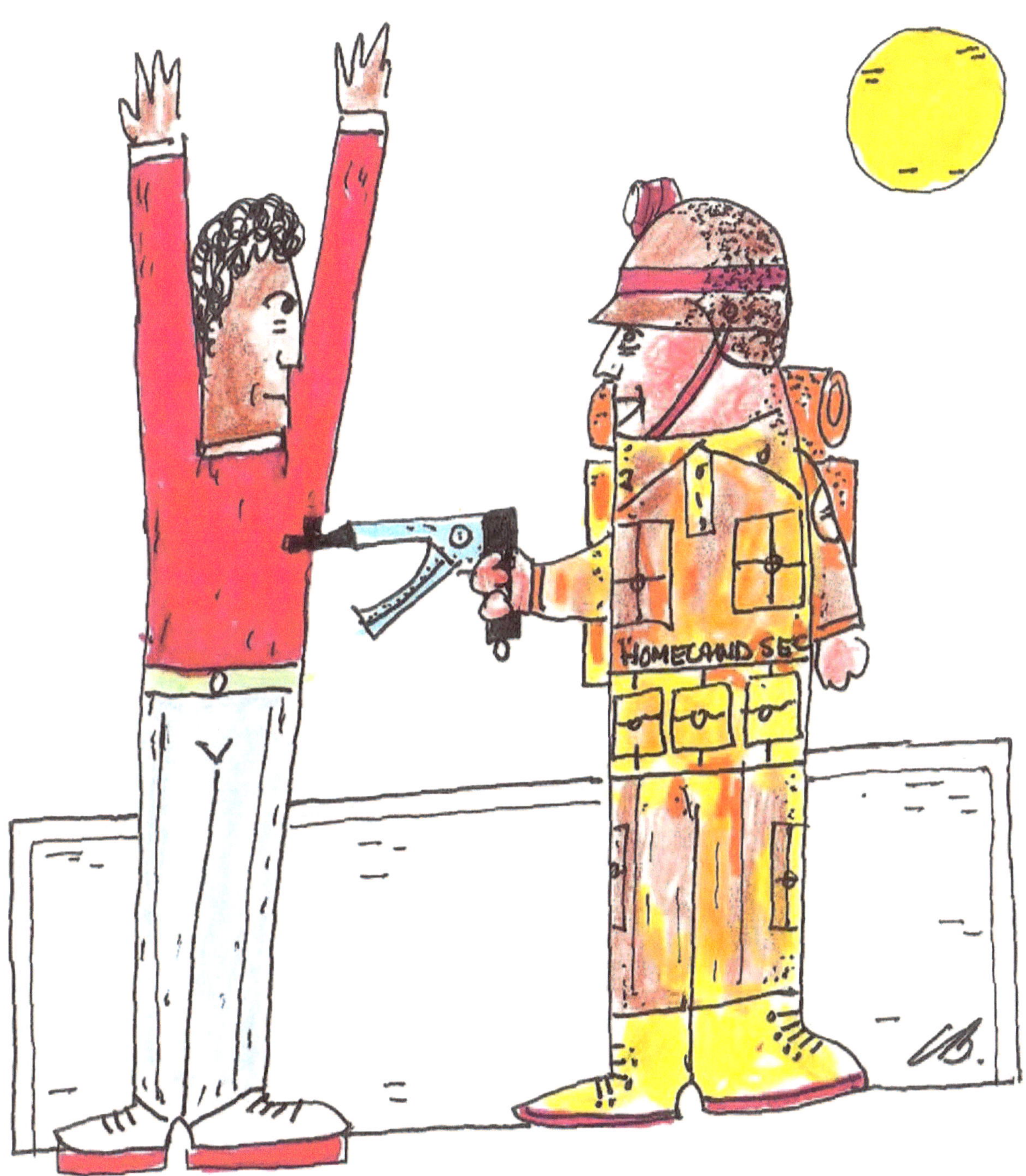

"I'm taking you in for looking swarthy!"

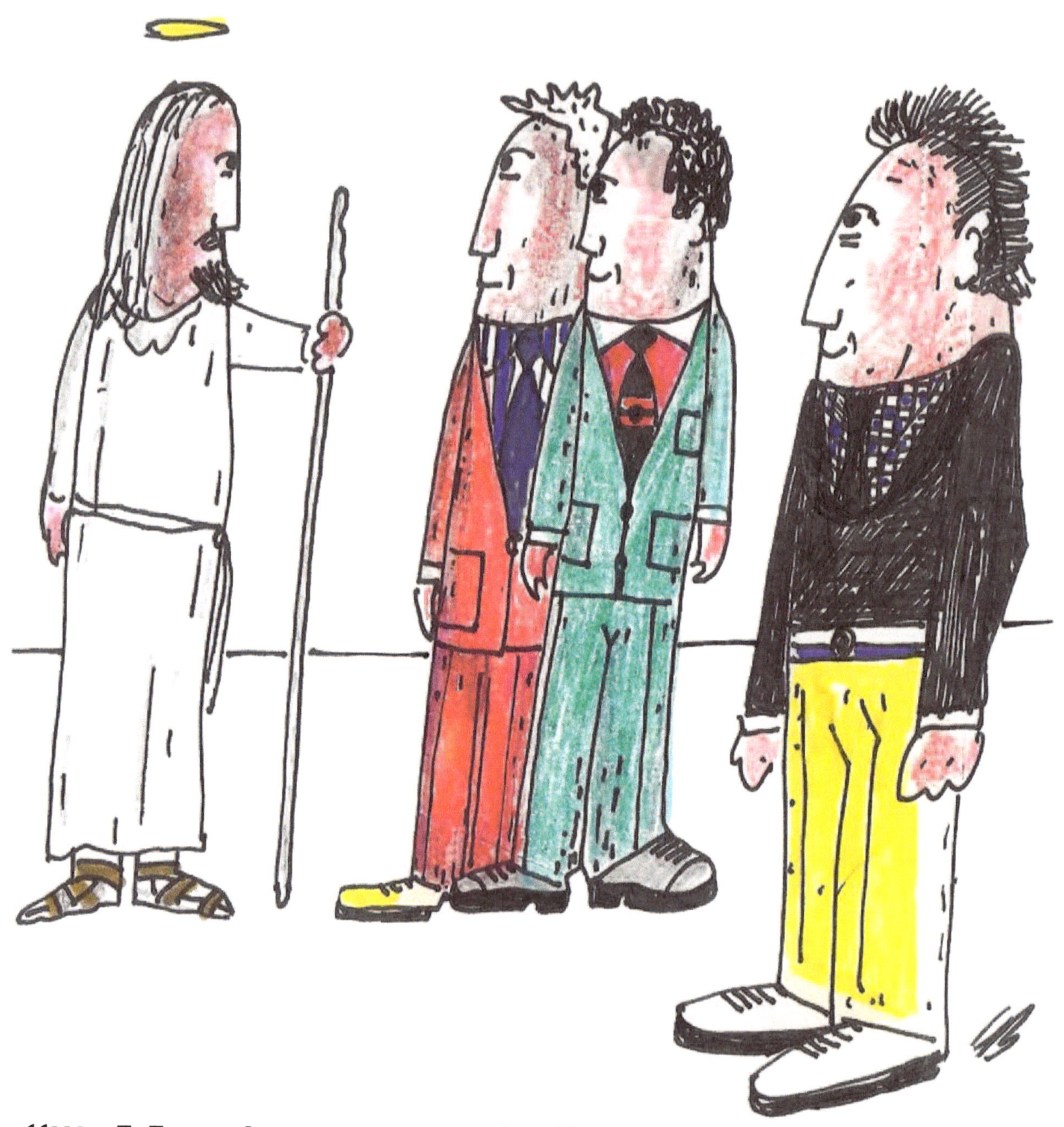

“Well, he certainly looks like a socialist!”

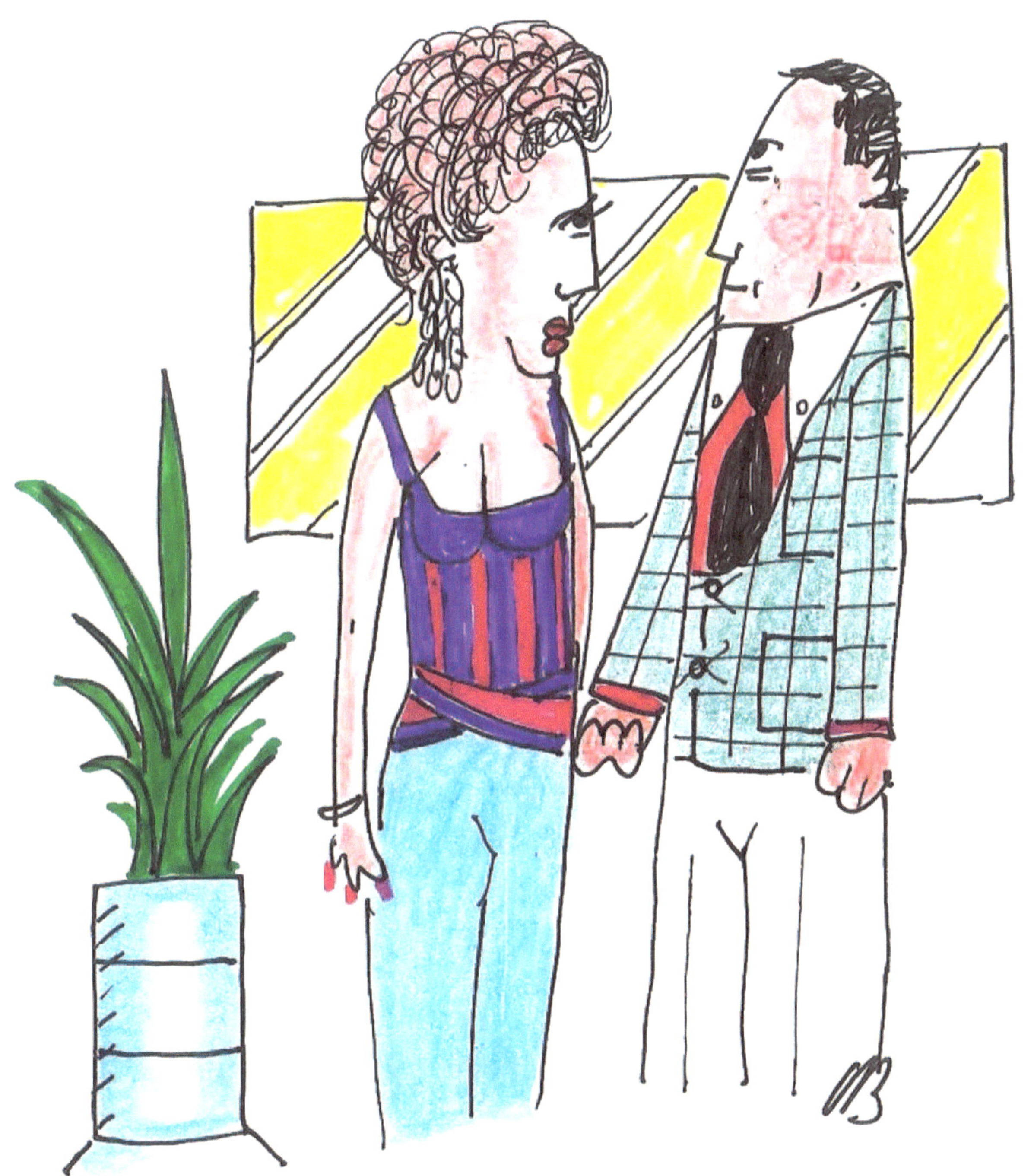

"I've been on the all green M &'Ms diet."

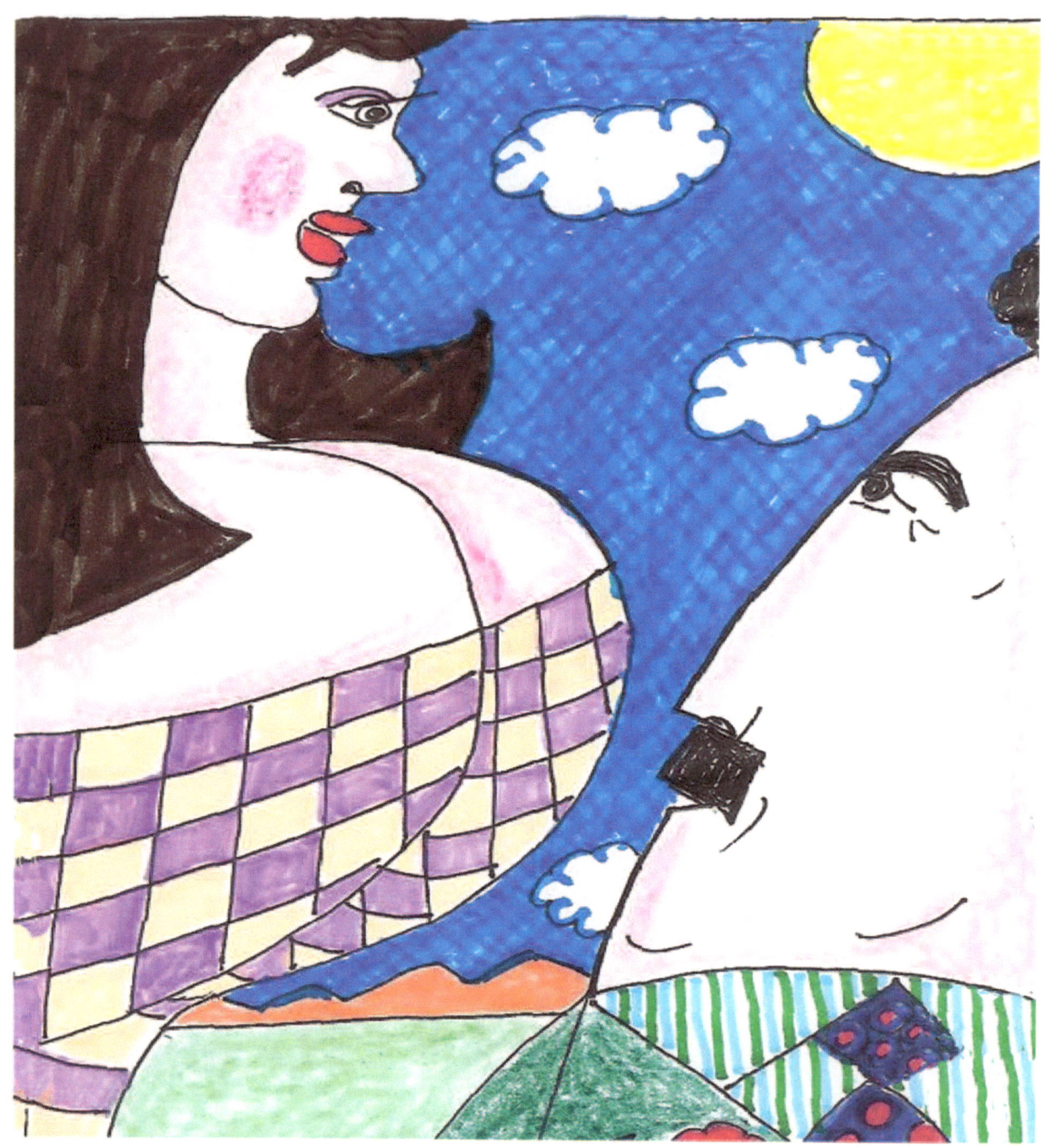

“Ralphie, I’m brimming over with the milk of human kindness.”

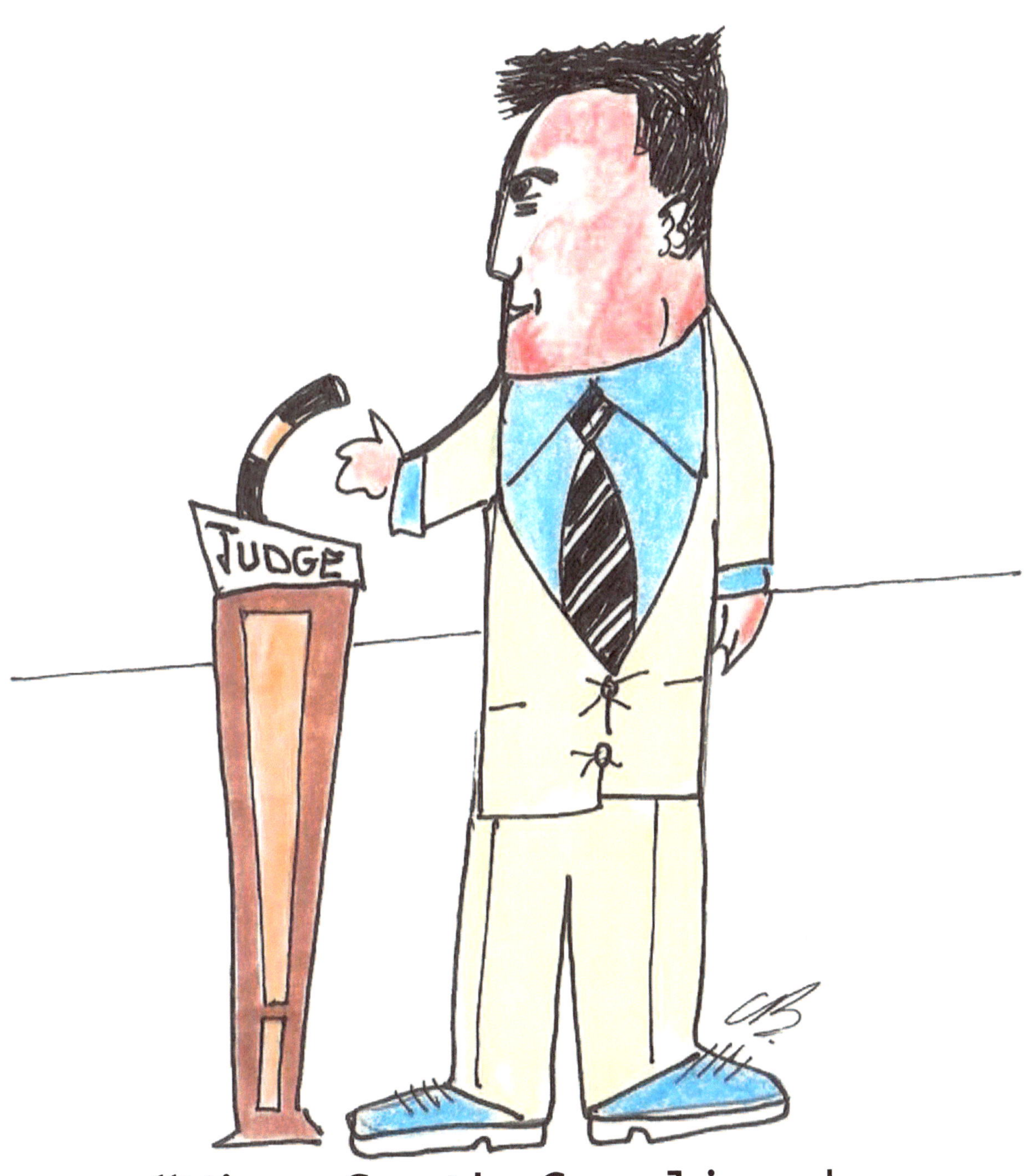

"Miss South Carolina has succumbed to a lack of long sentences."

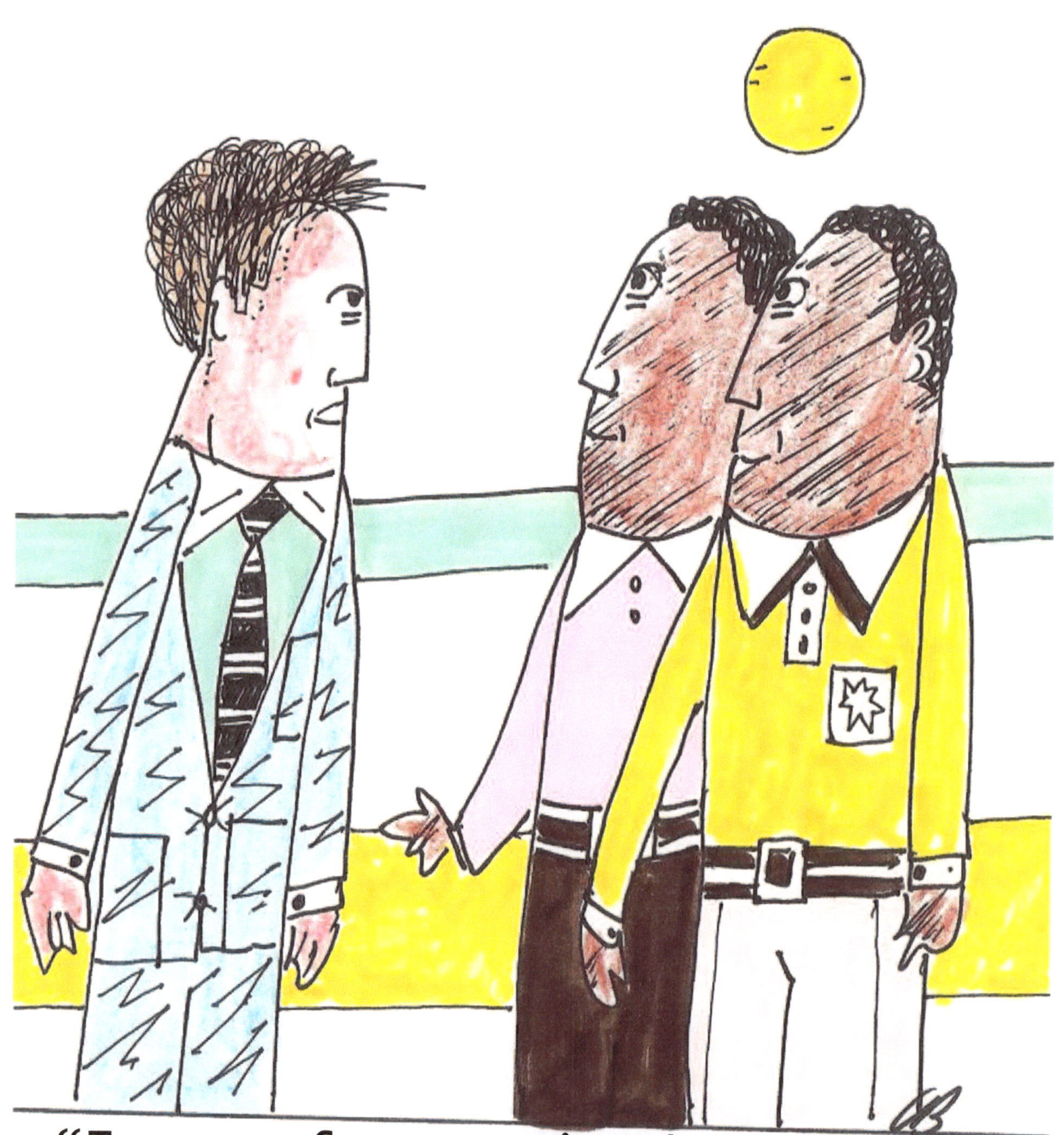

“I come from a mixed marriage. Dad was a drunk. Mom was a tweeker.”

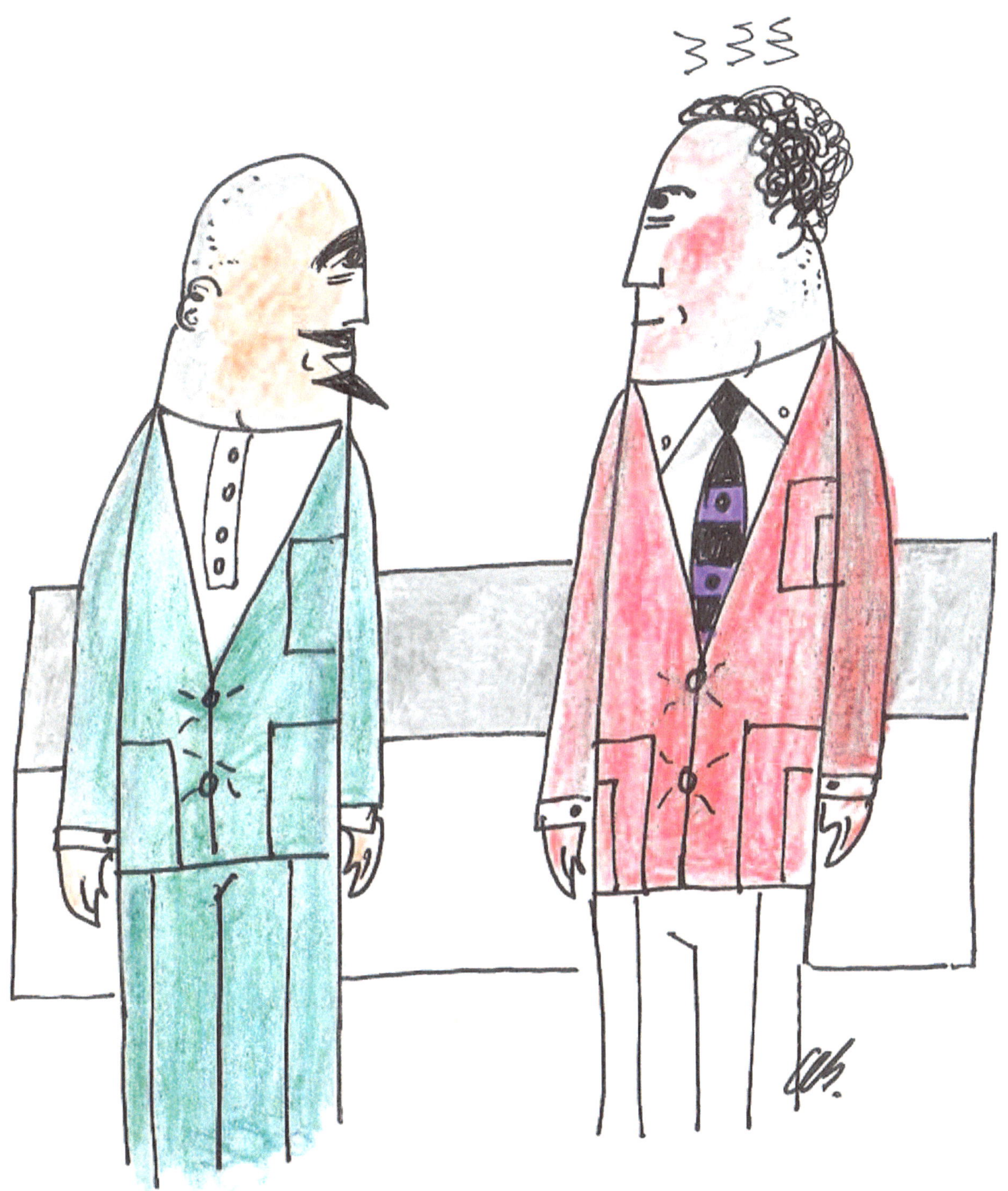

“We’re putting a Mosque in our local Wal-Mart.”

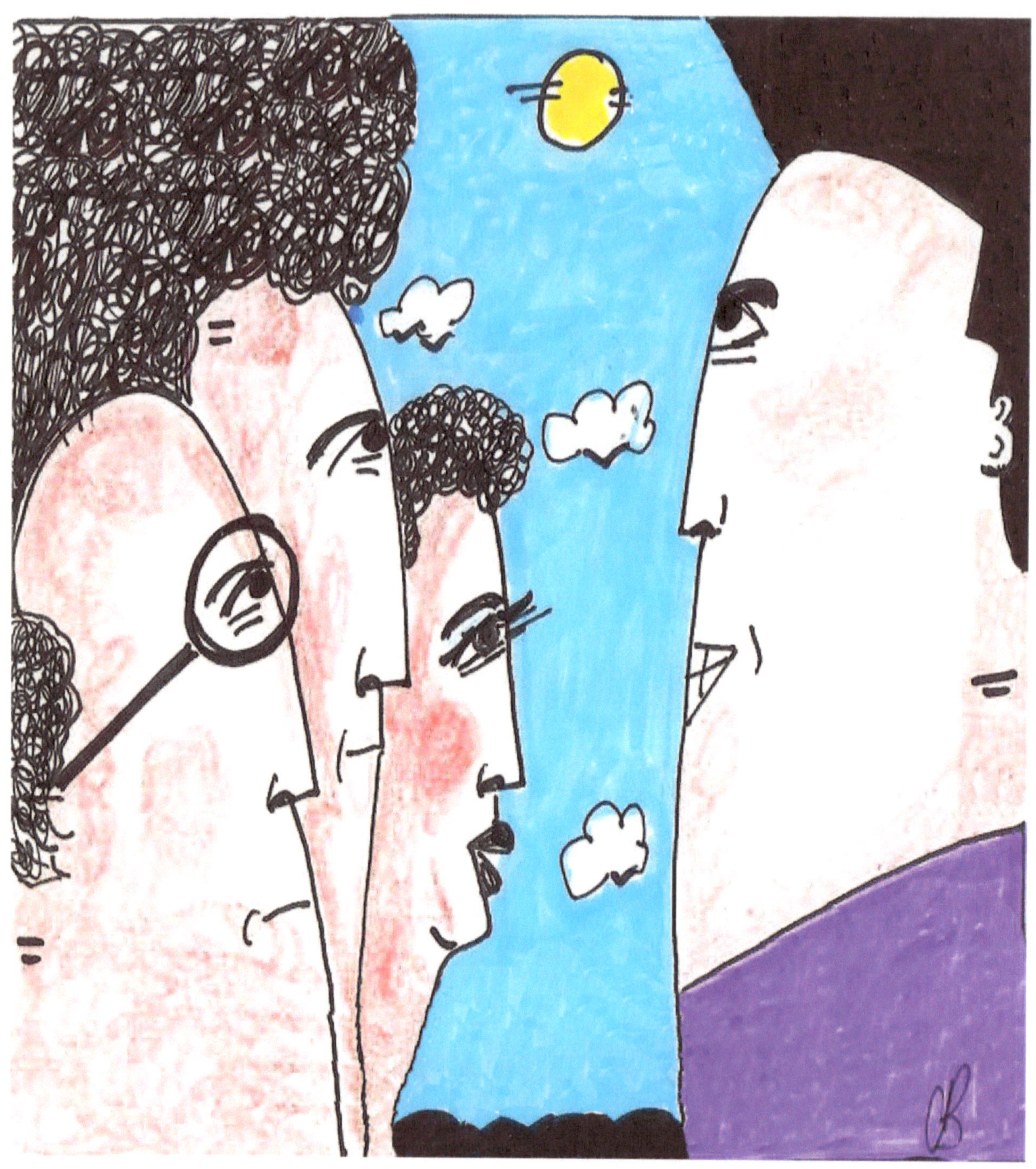

"Okay staff, no more three ways on lunch break."

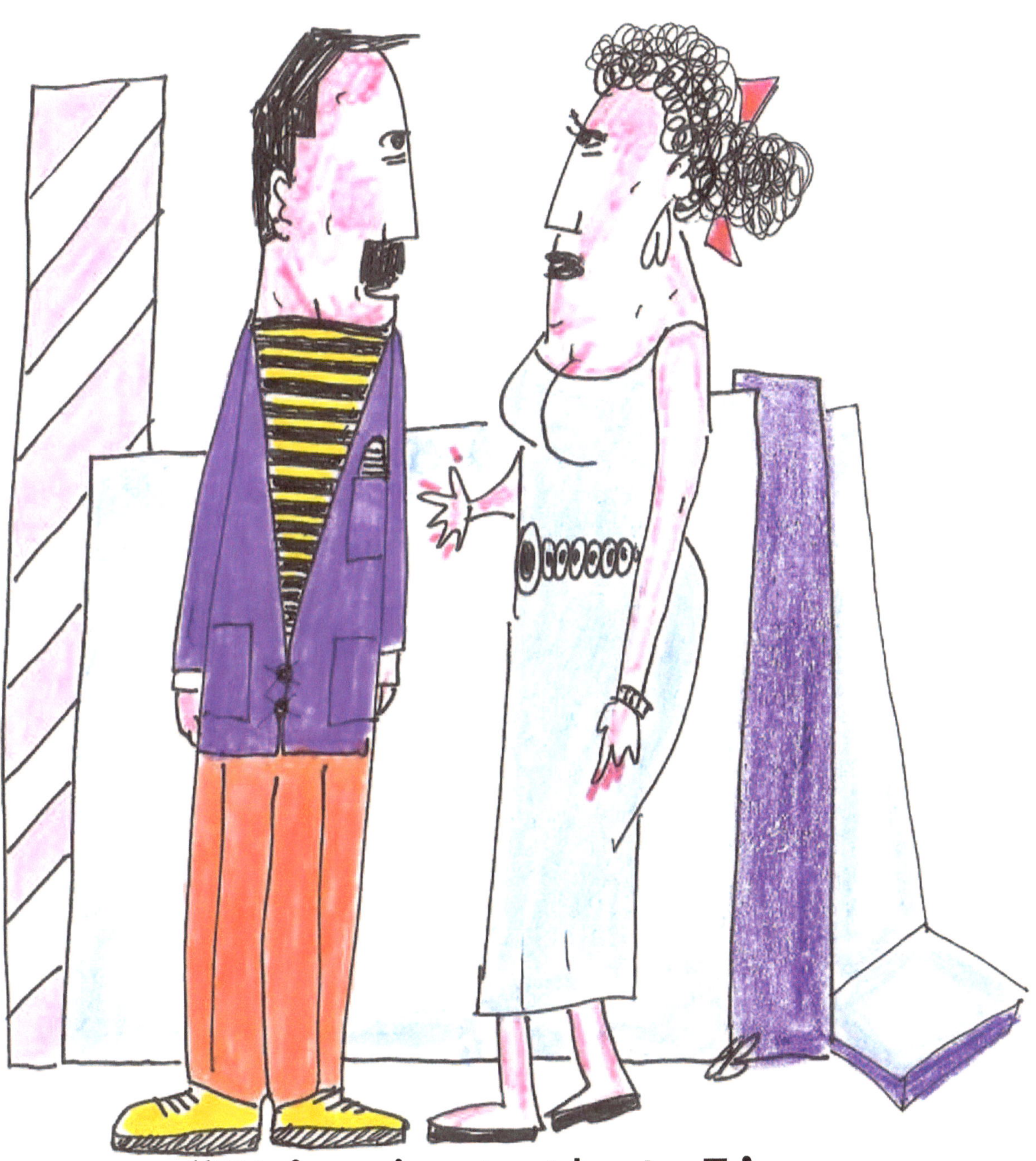

“It’s just that I’m a renaissance man, and you watch Fox News.”

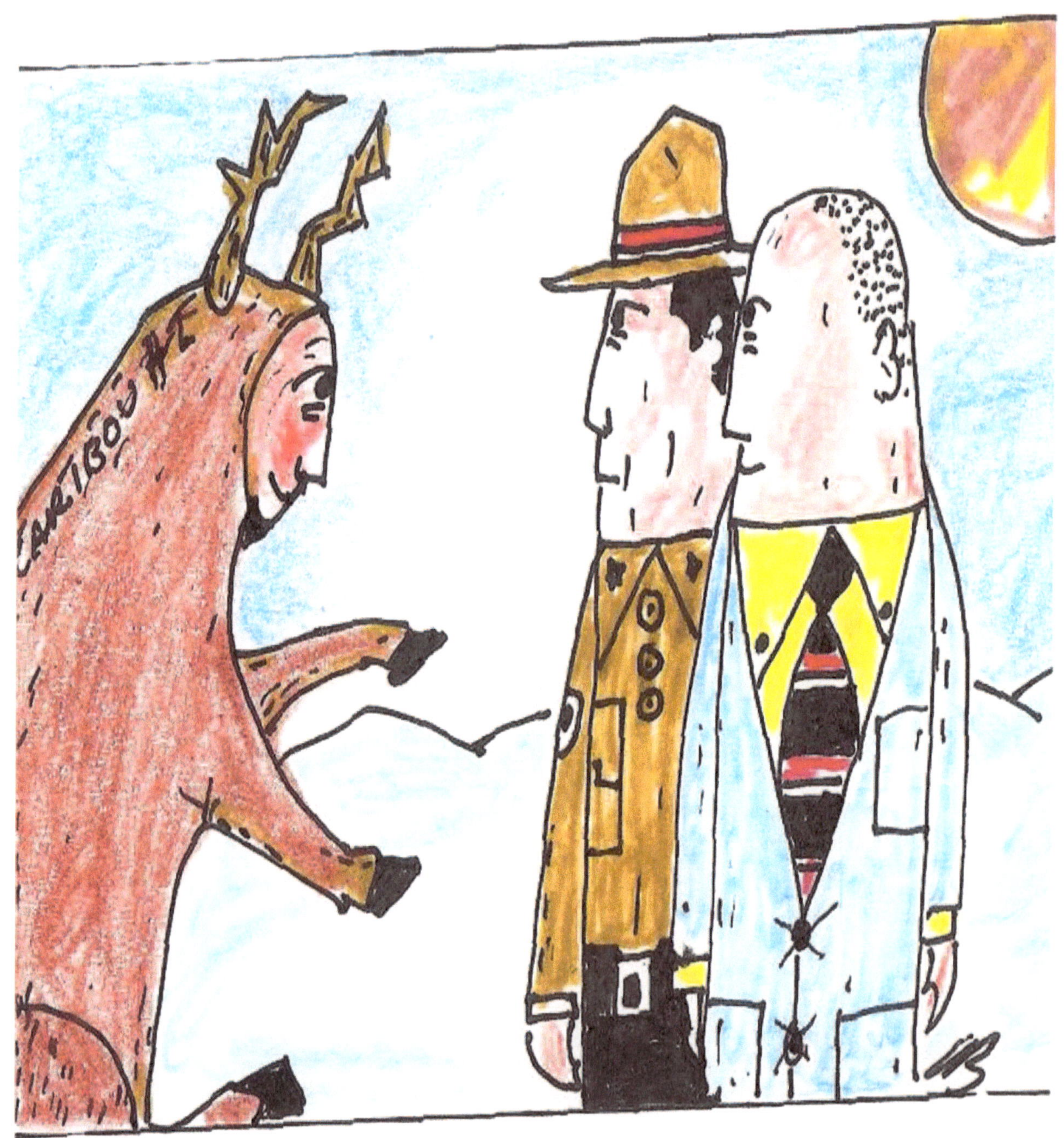

"He's a reporter from MSNBC doing a story on Sarah Palin."

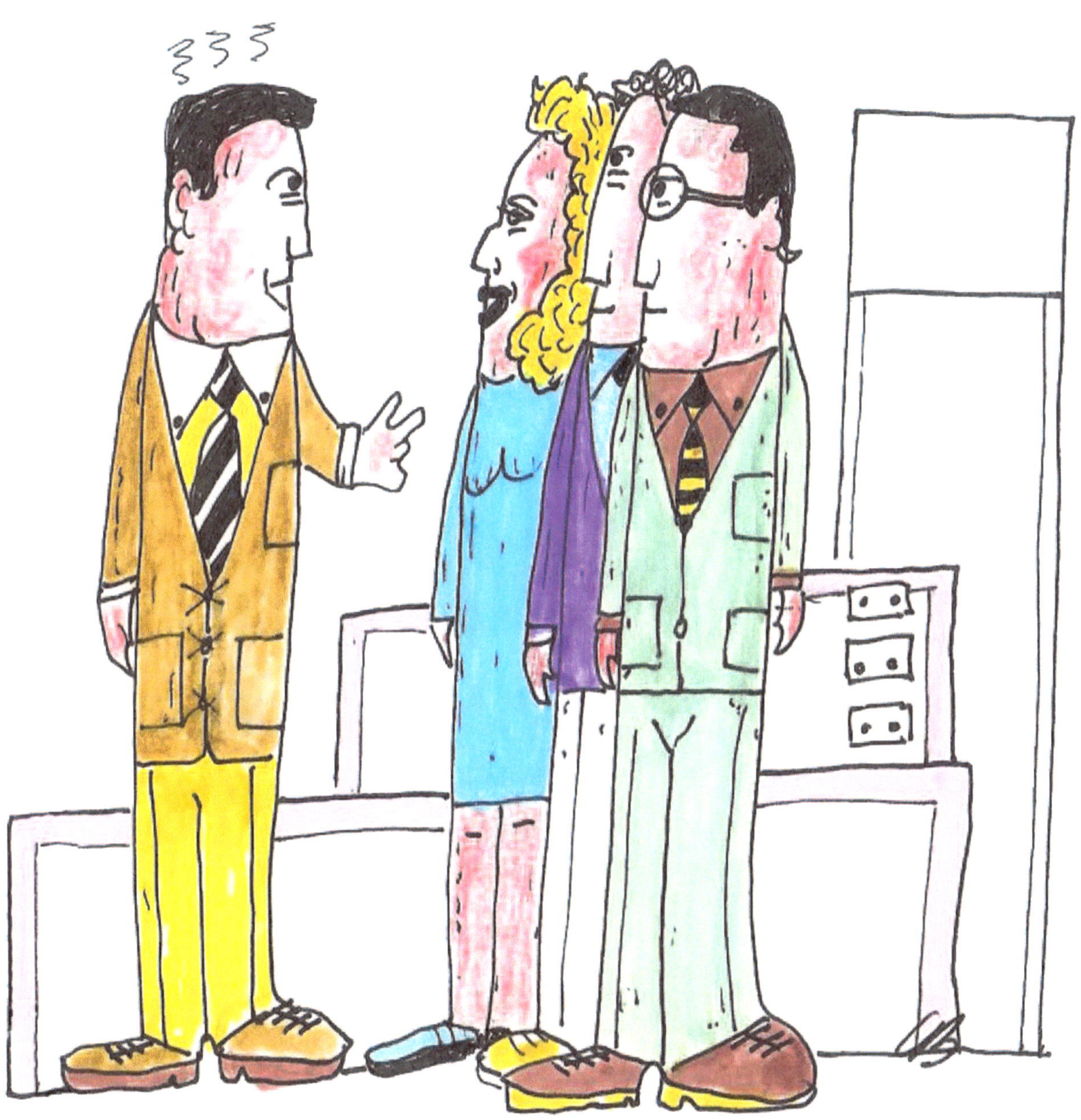

“I had sex with my text!”

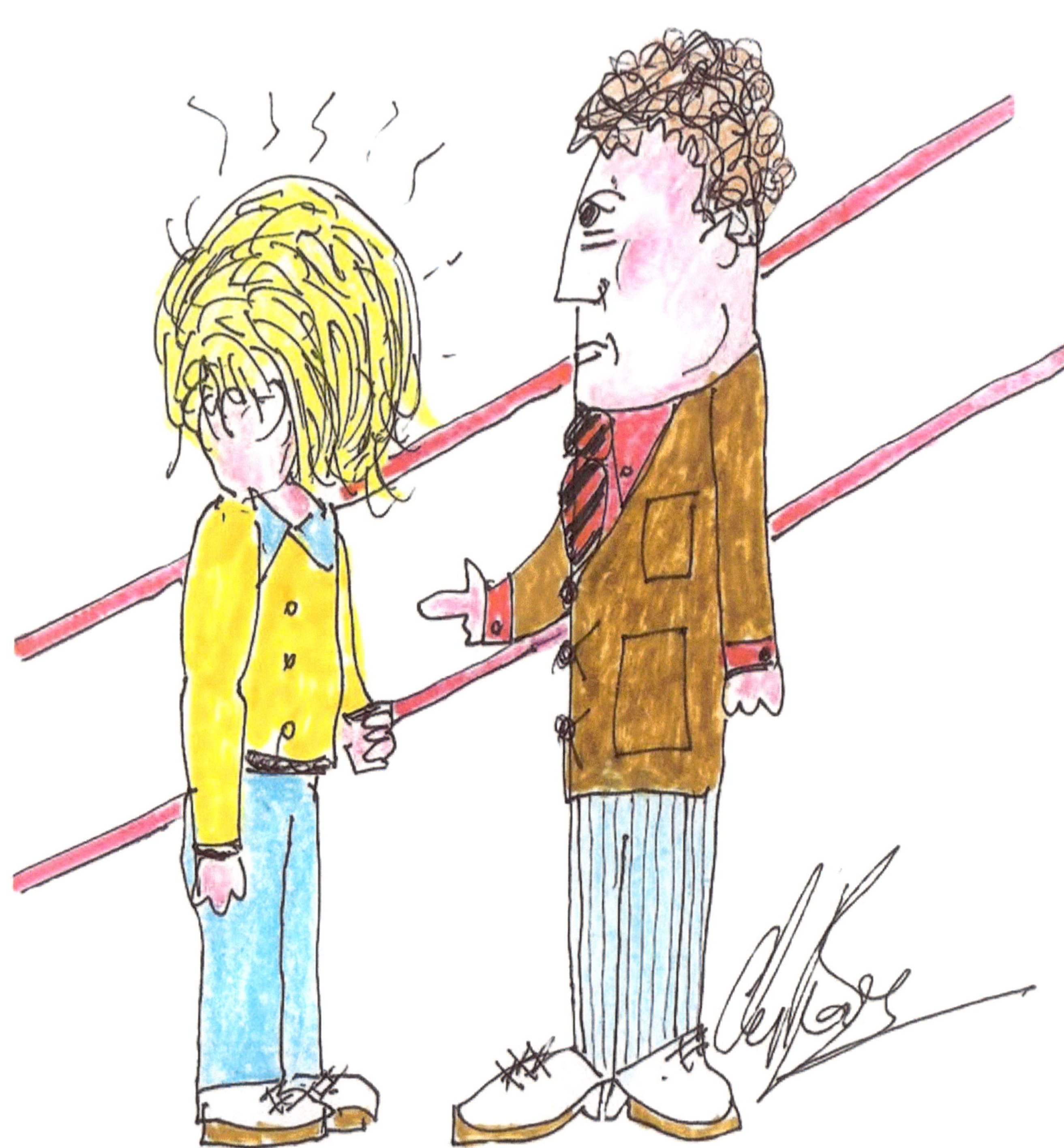

"So why should I believe you're Donald Trump's son?"

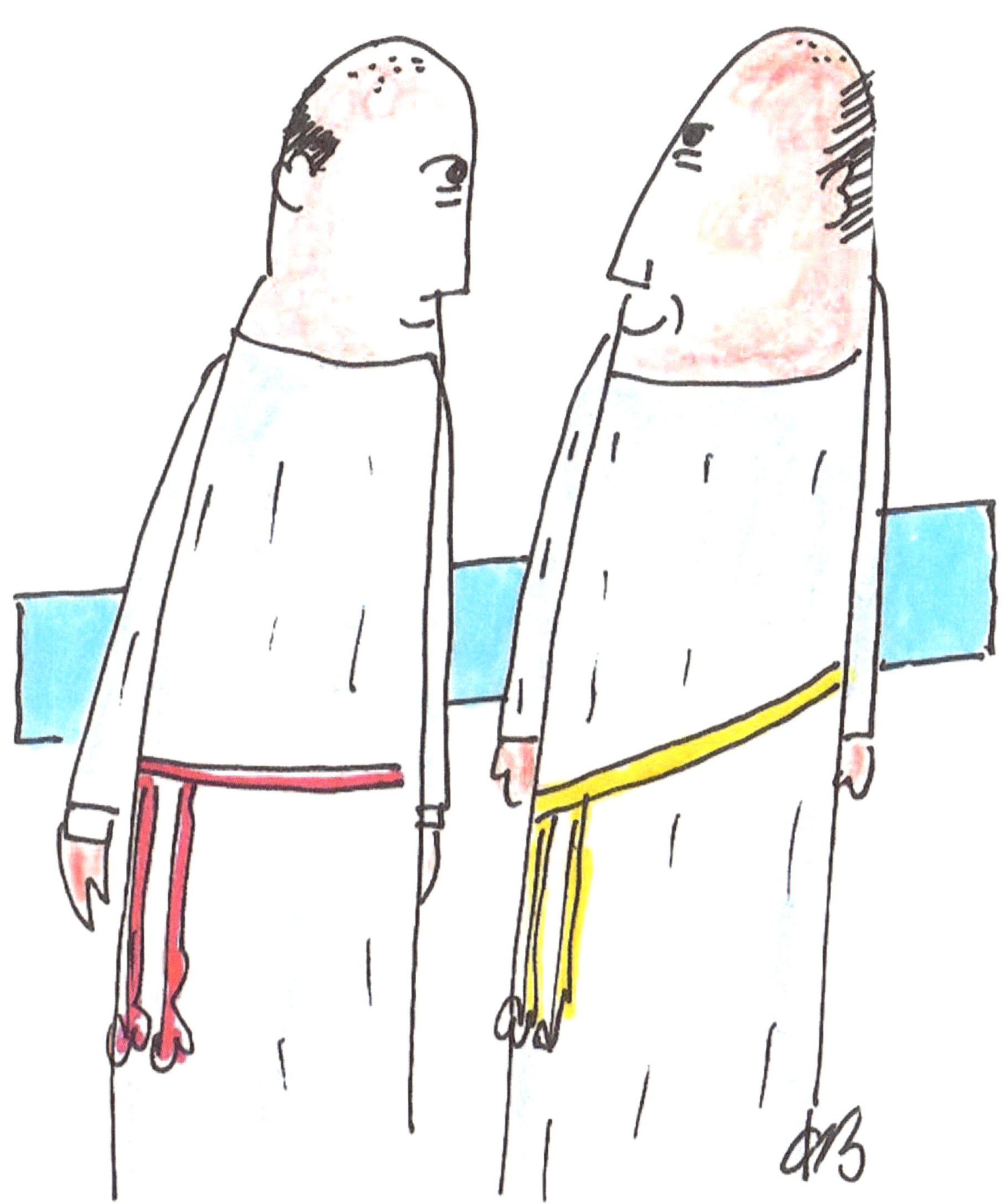

"That's funny...you don't look Trappist."

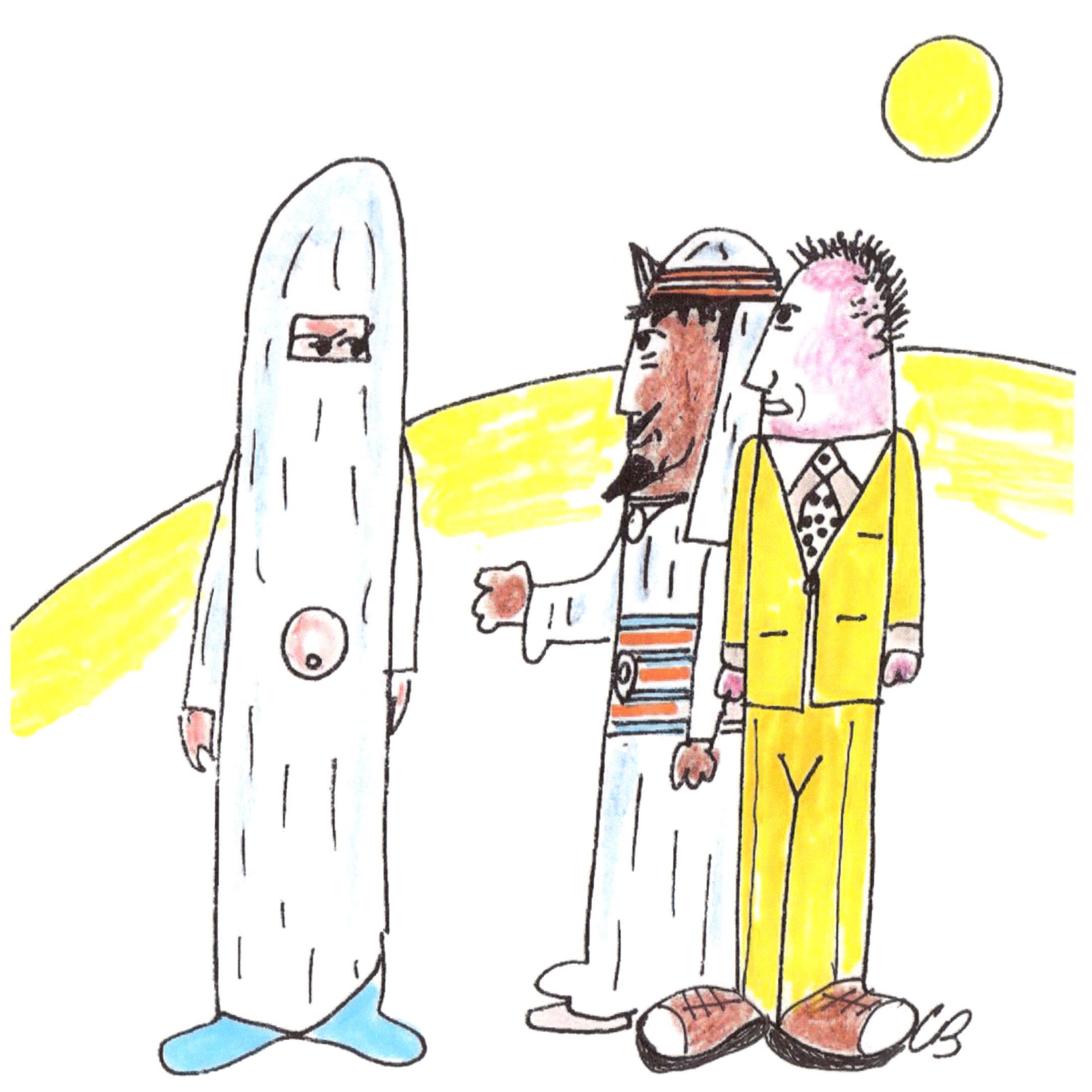

"Your Majestly, may I present...
Cher."

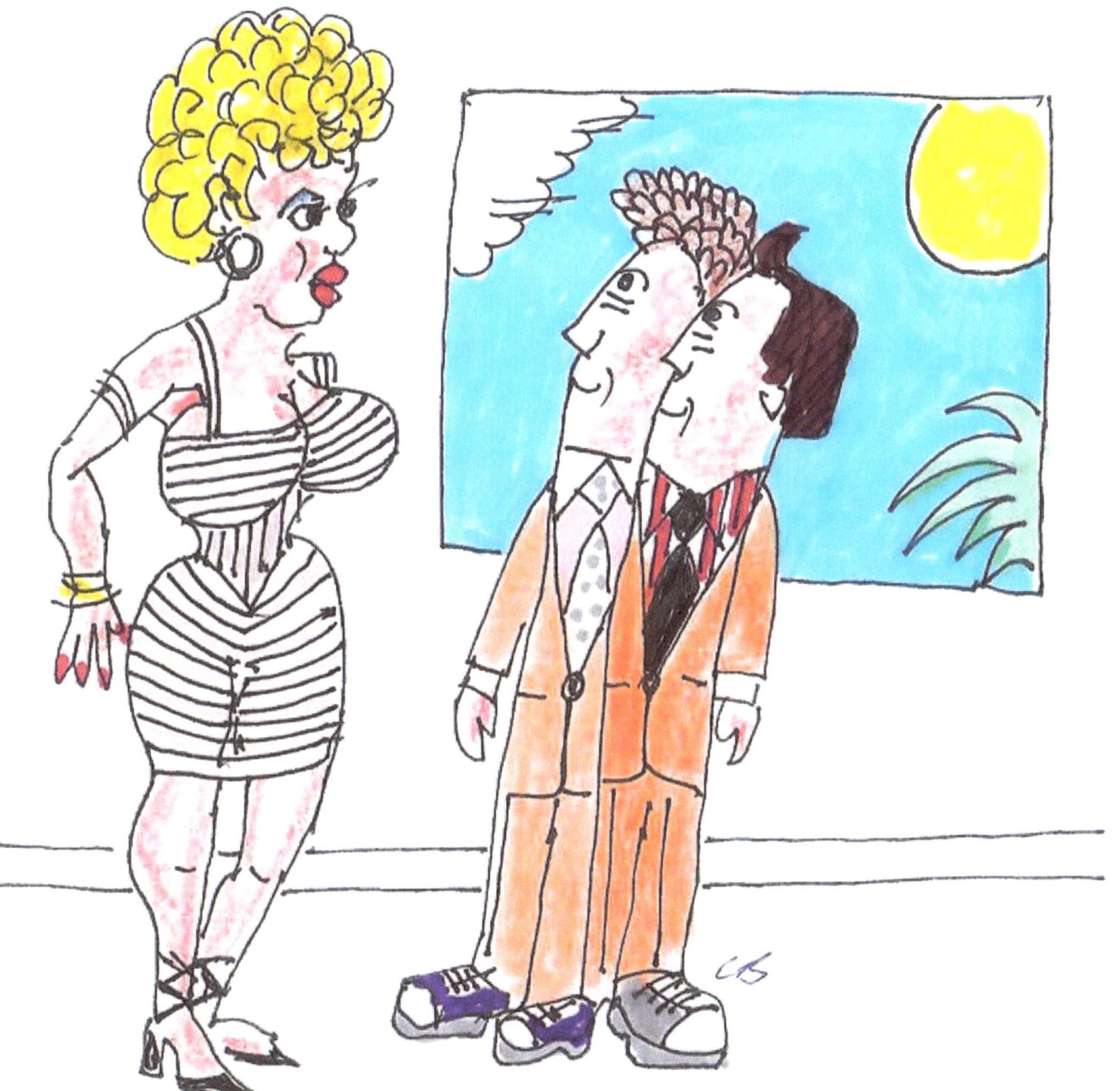

"Here it is Roger, fresh from the factory...The first Giant Fox News Slut."

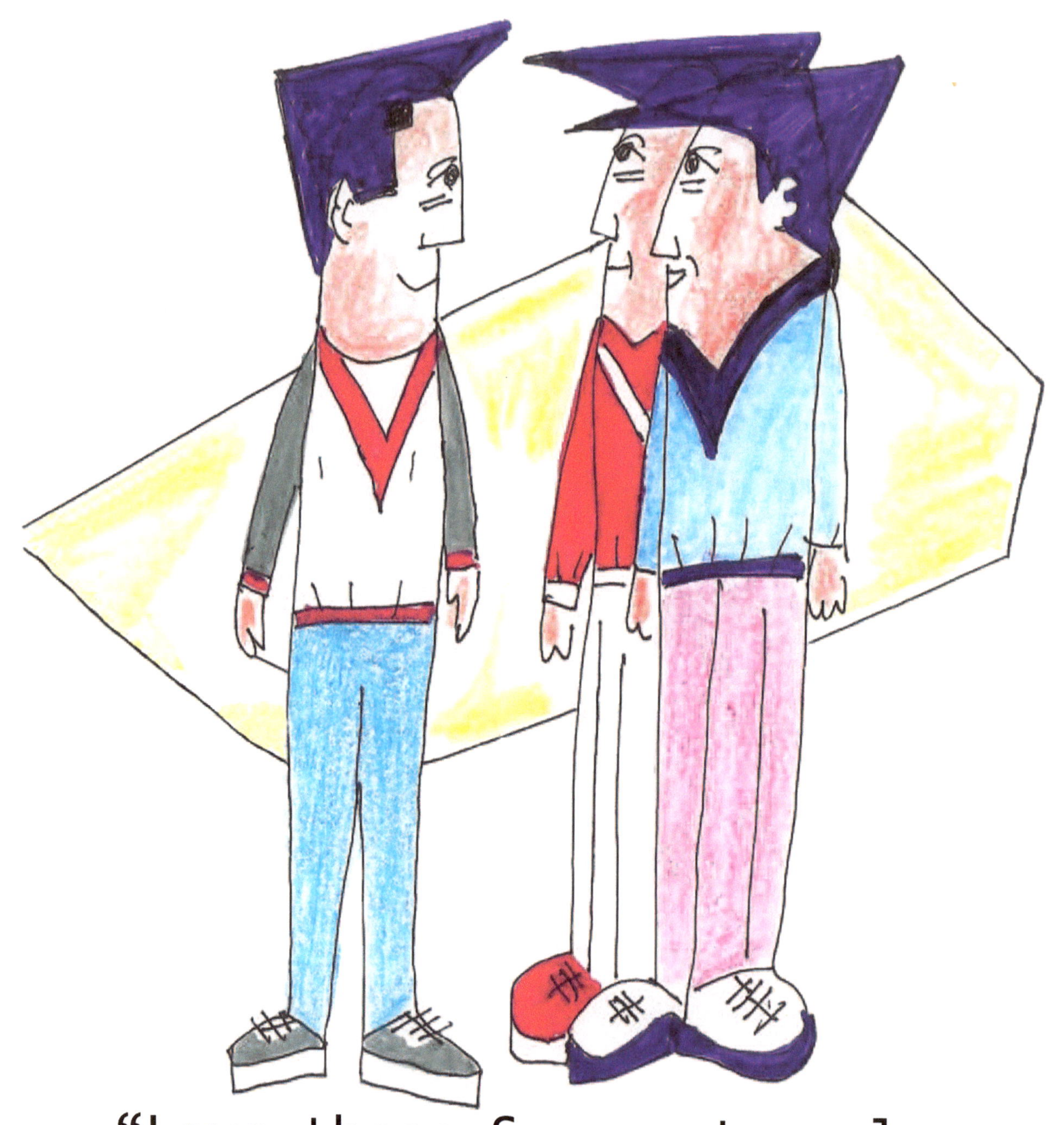

"Love those Supercuts sale days."

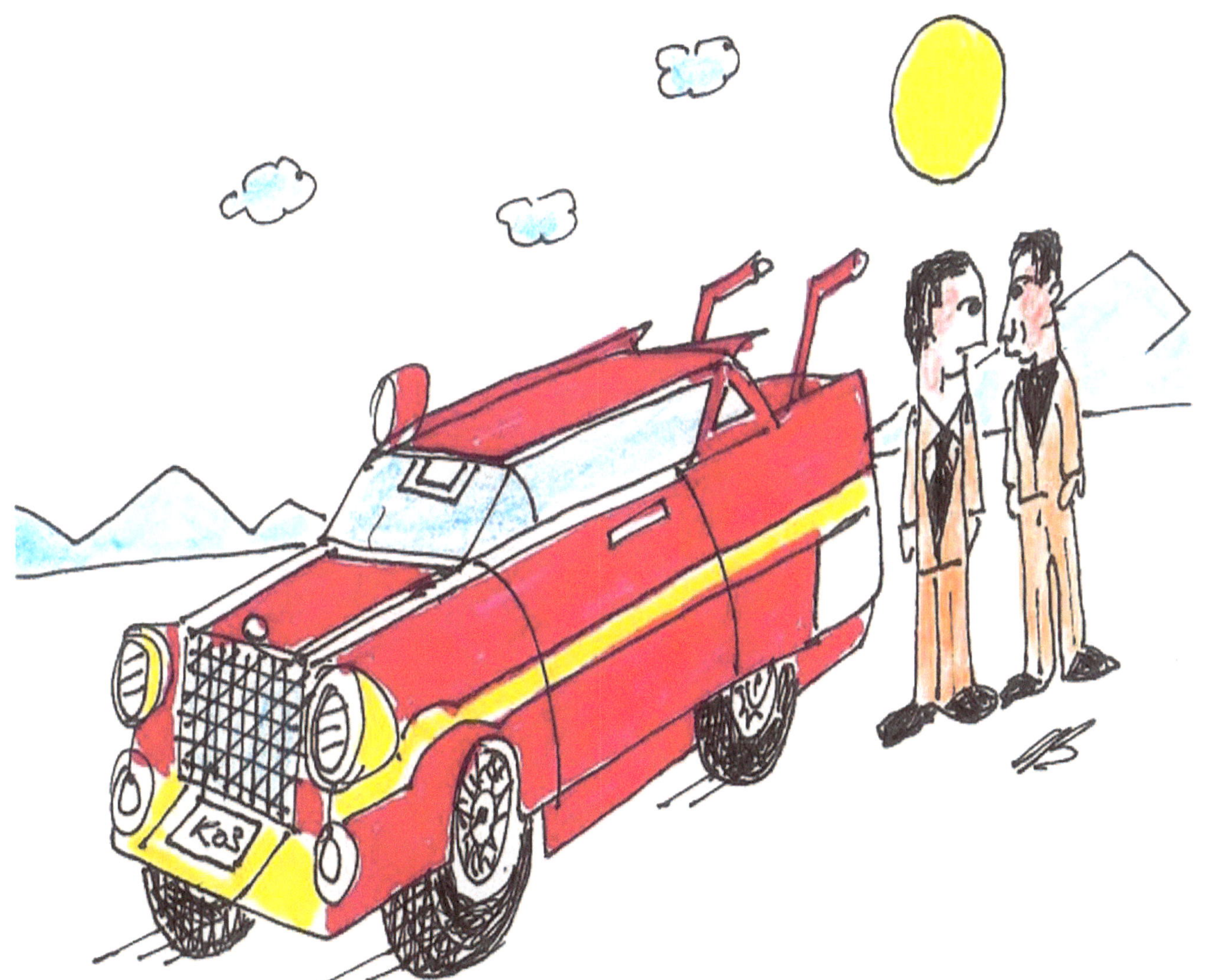

"This is a Lithuanian Hybrid,
made entirely of spare parts."

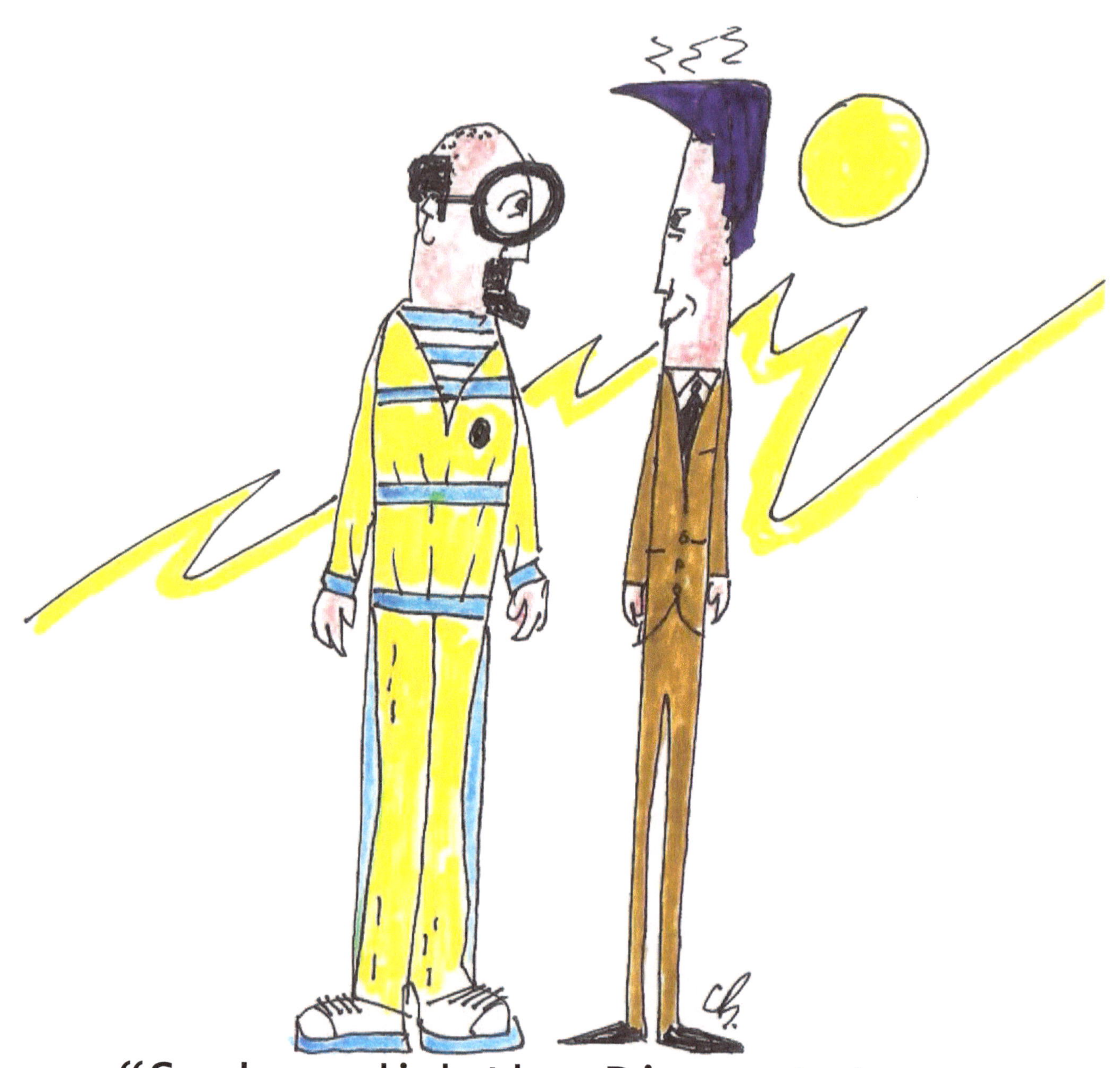

“So how did the Biggest Loser audition go, Phil?”

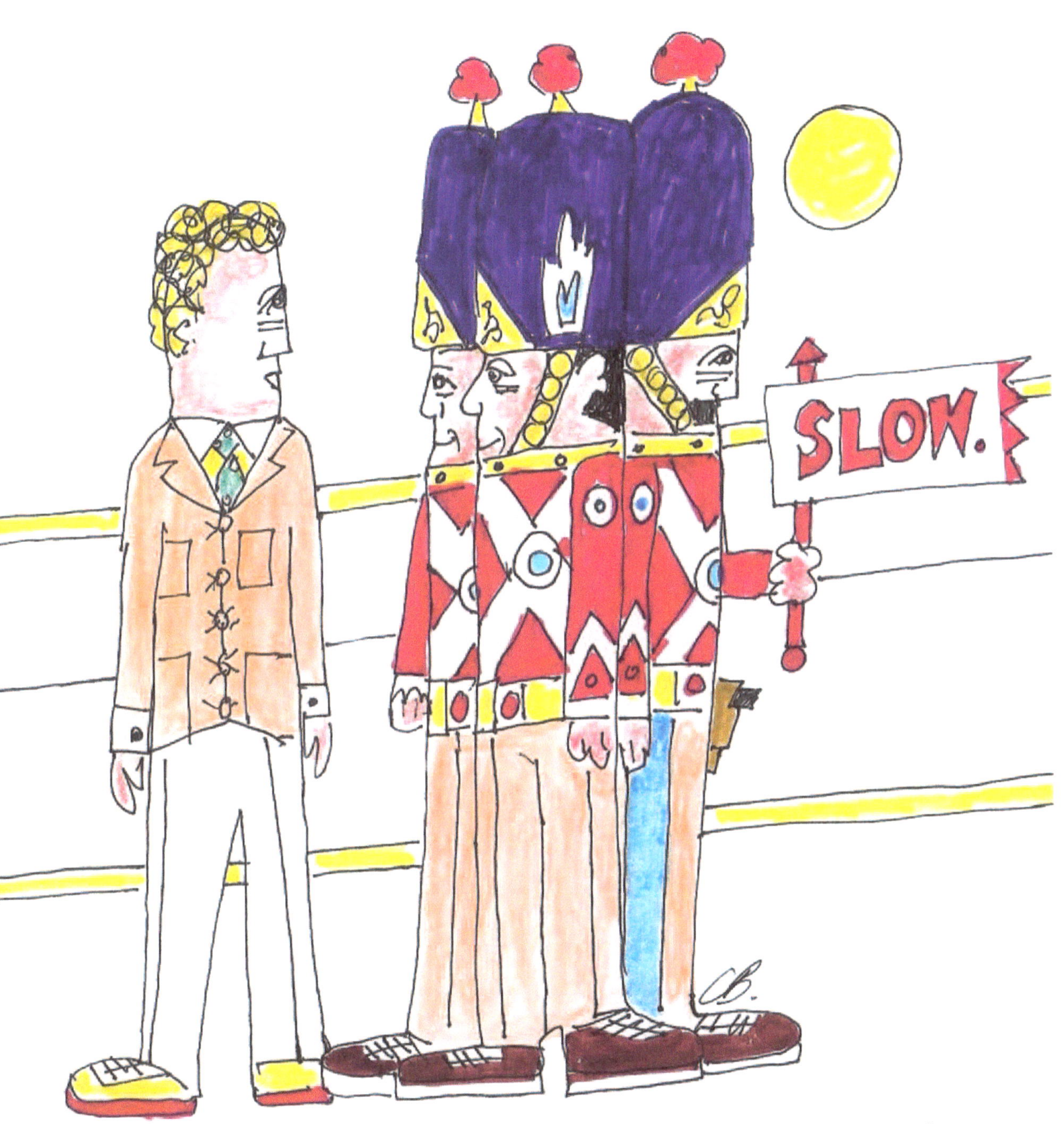

“These new uniforms seem to be a little much for the Arizona Highway Patrol.”

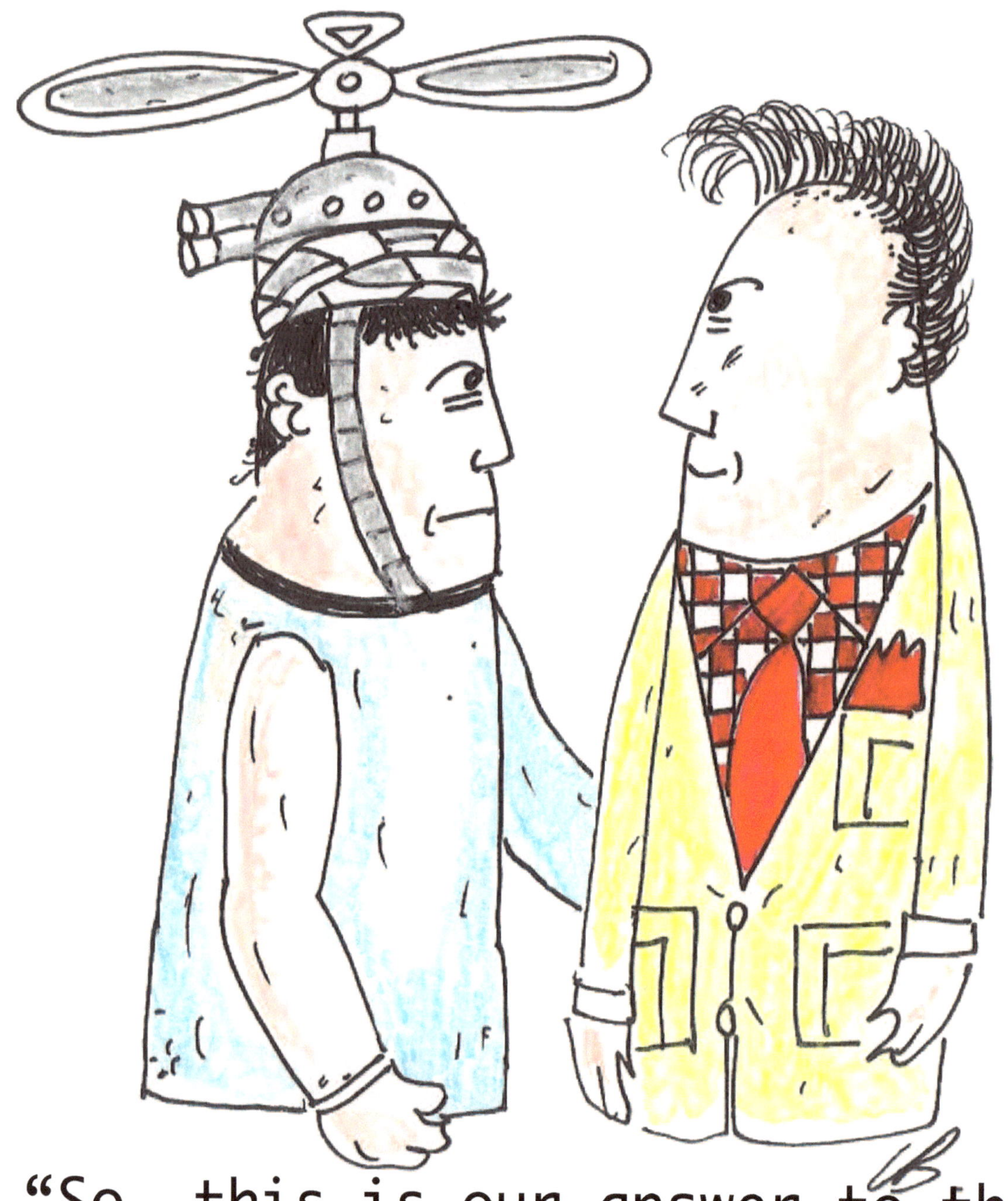

“So, this is our answer to the Prius?”

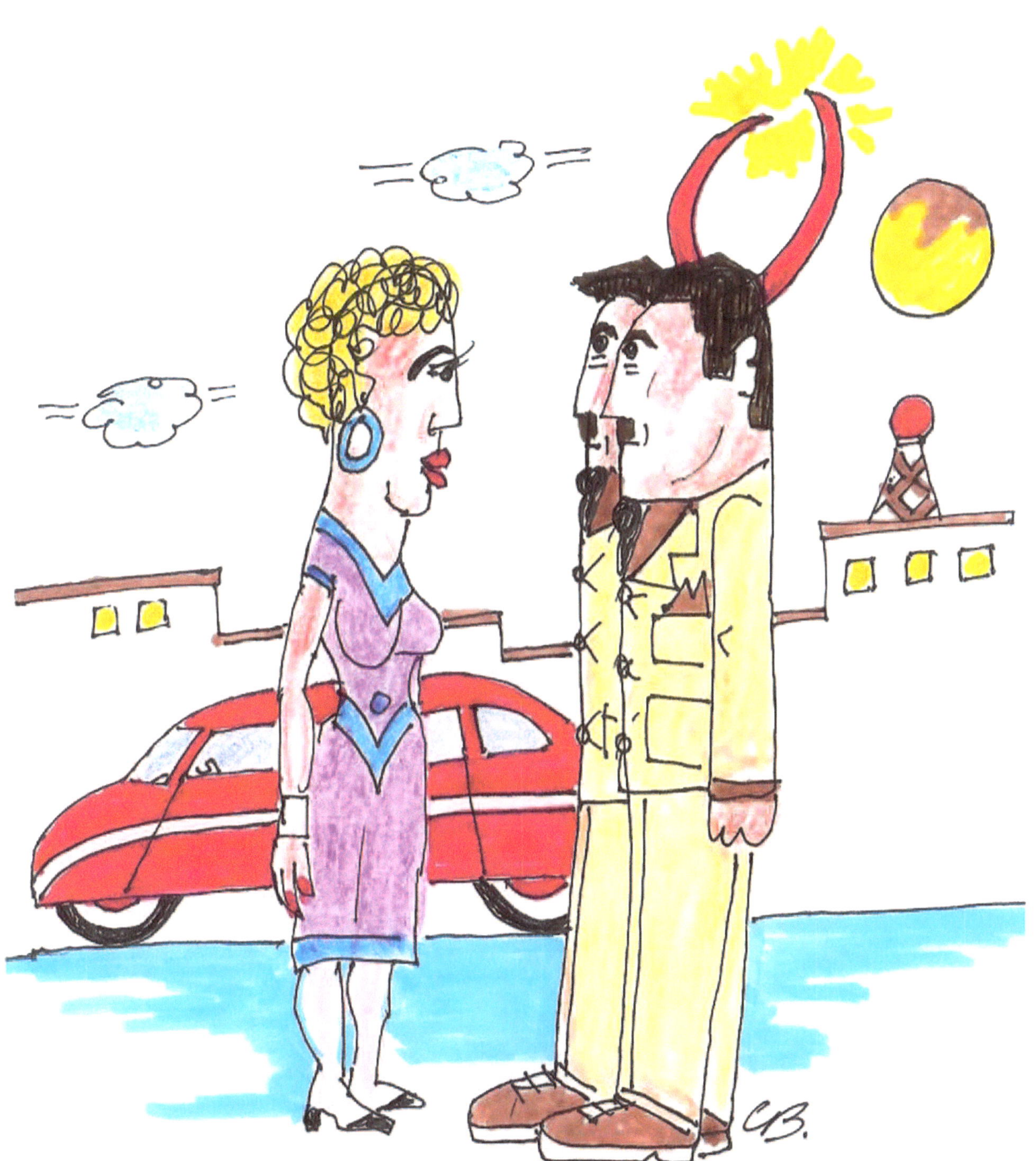

"I'll bet you can't tell which one's the evil twin."

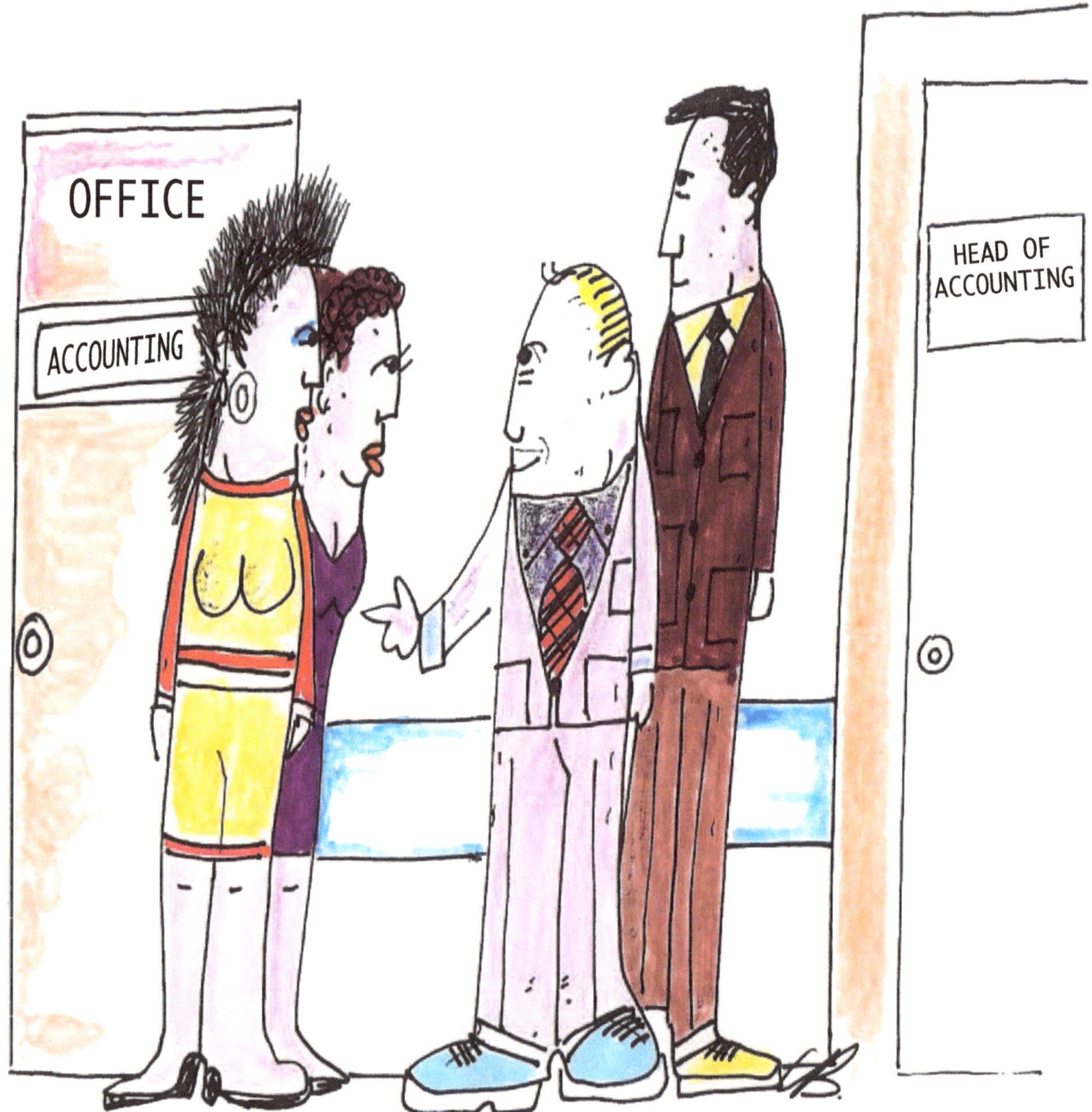

"You girls want to have sex in the city, or wait until the Blue Ridge Mountains?"

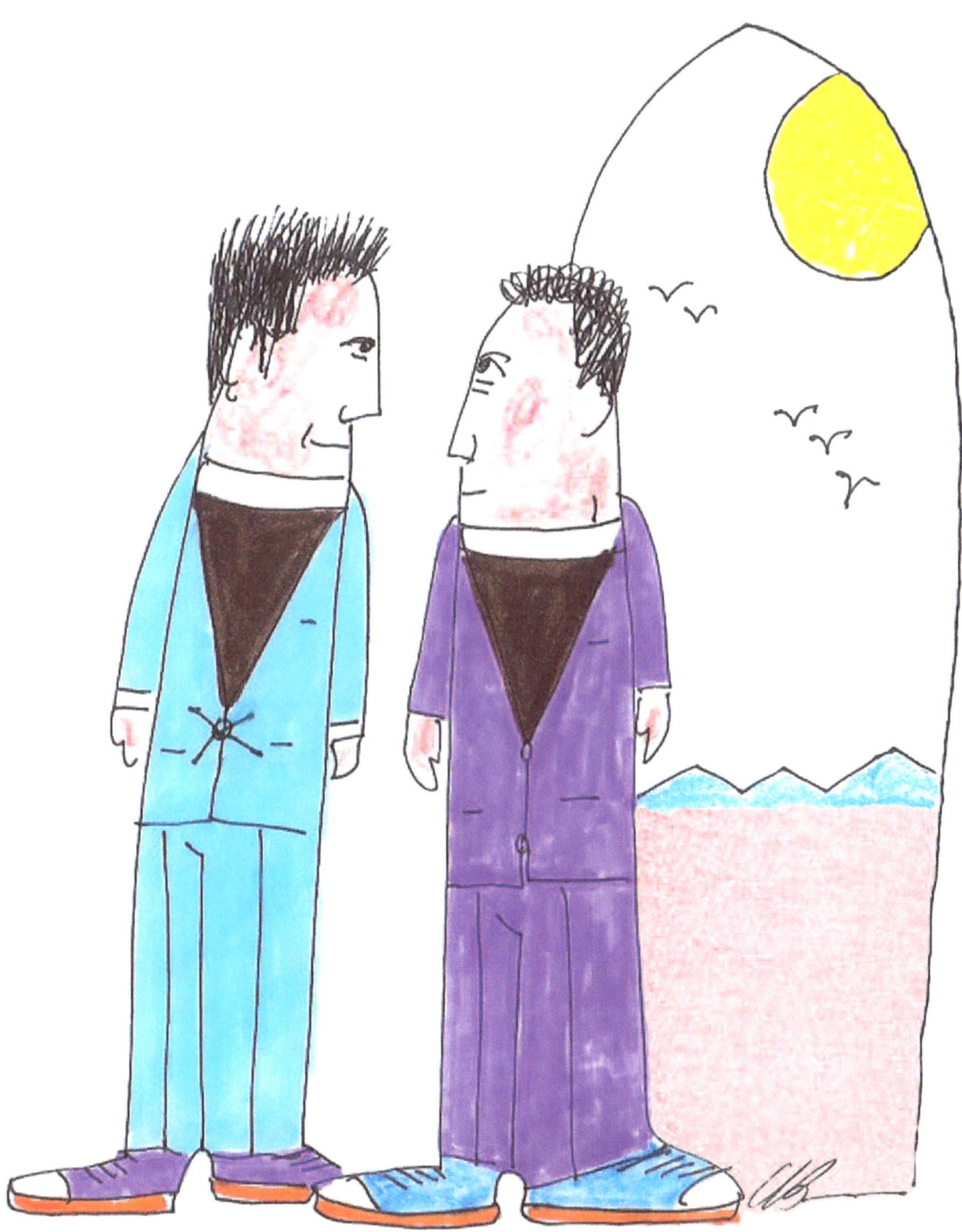

“Wanna go out tonight and celebate?”

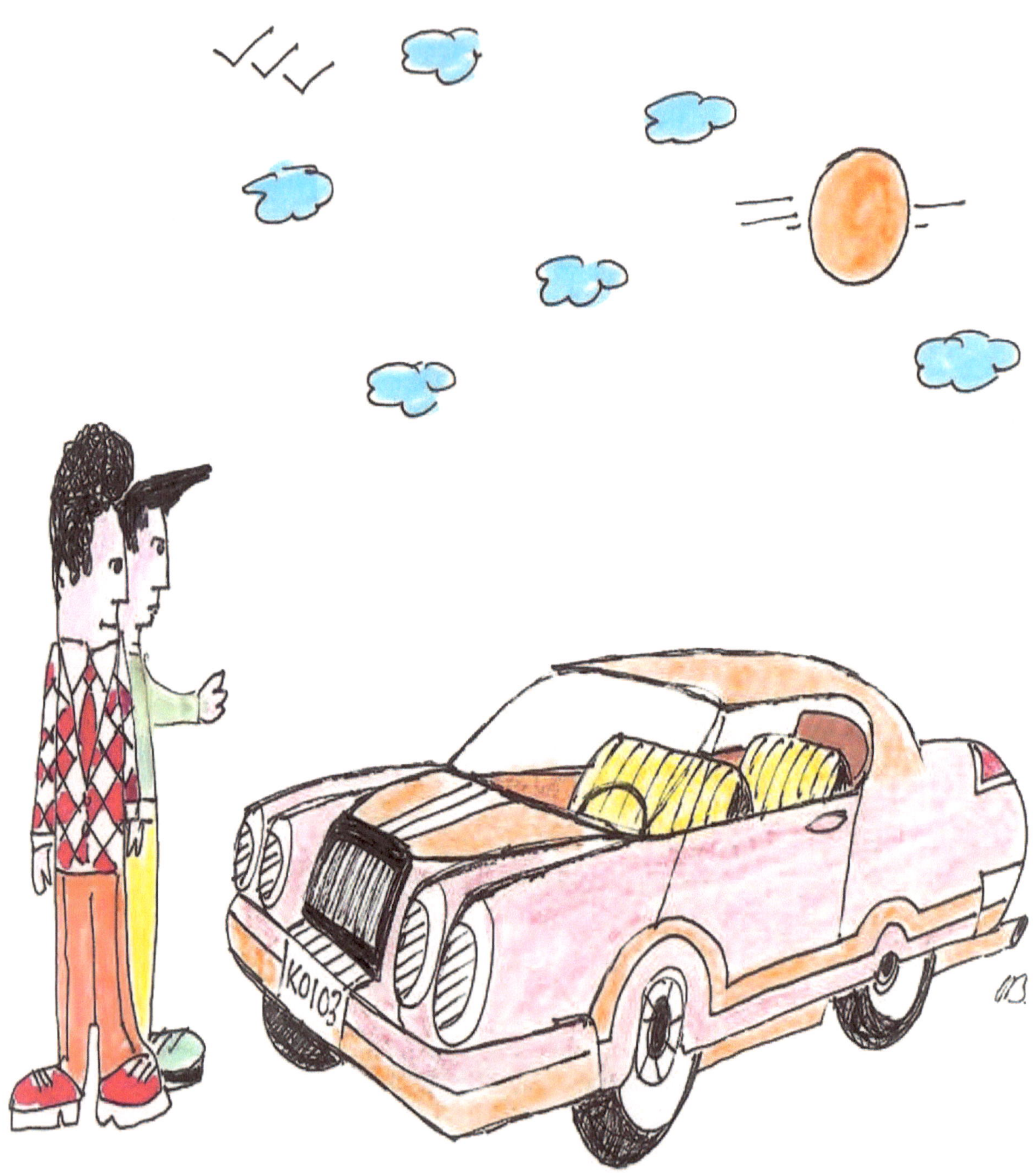

"This motor runs entirely on contaminated gulf shrimp."

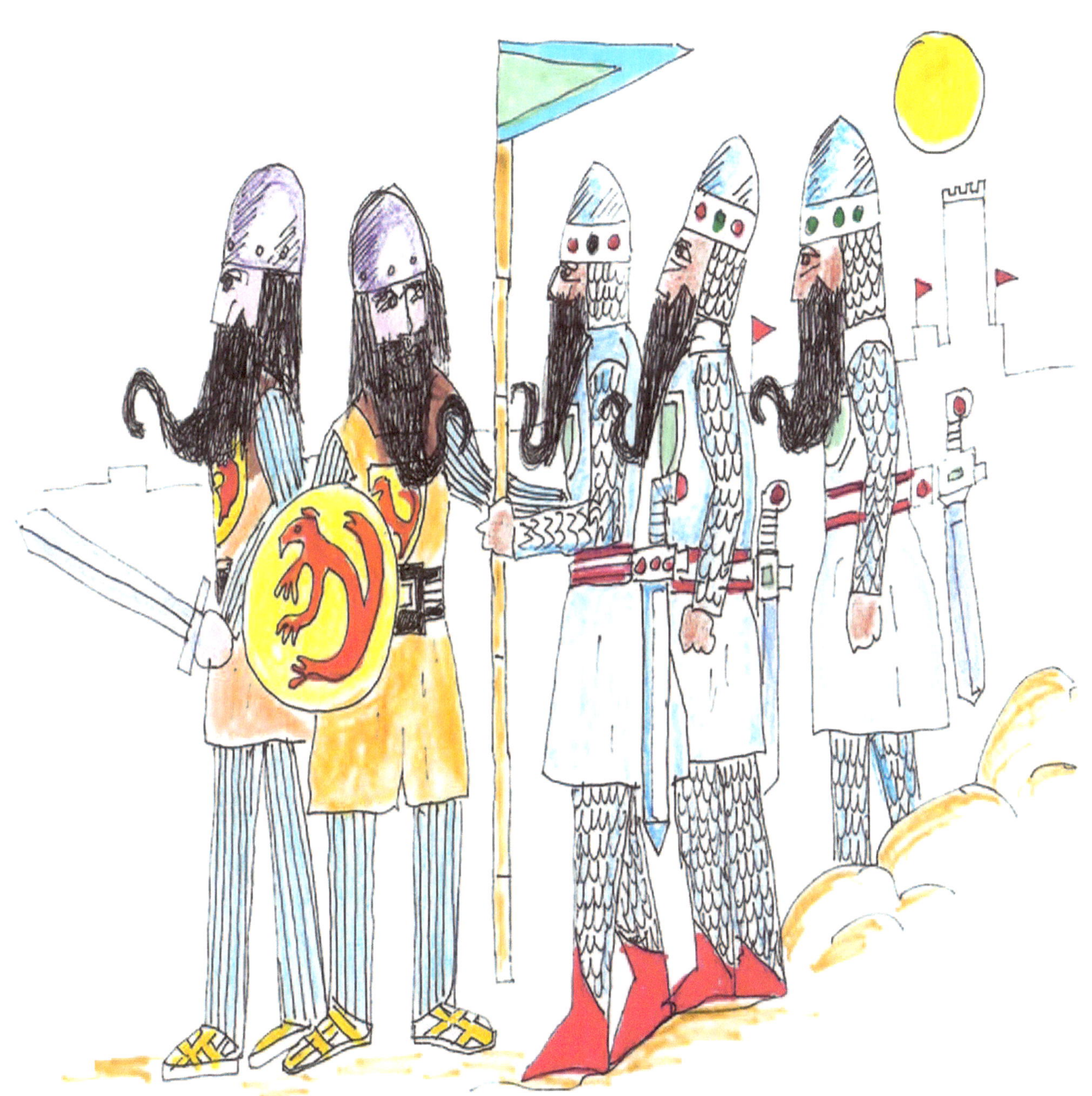

“So that’s where Pierre the stylist went...Islam.”

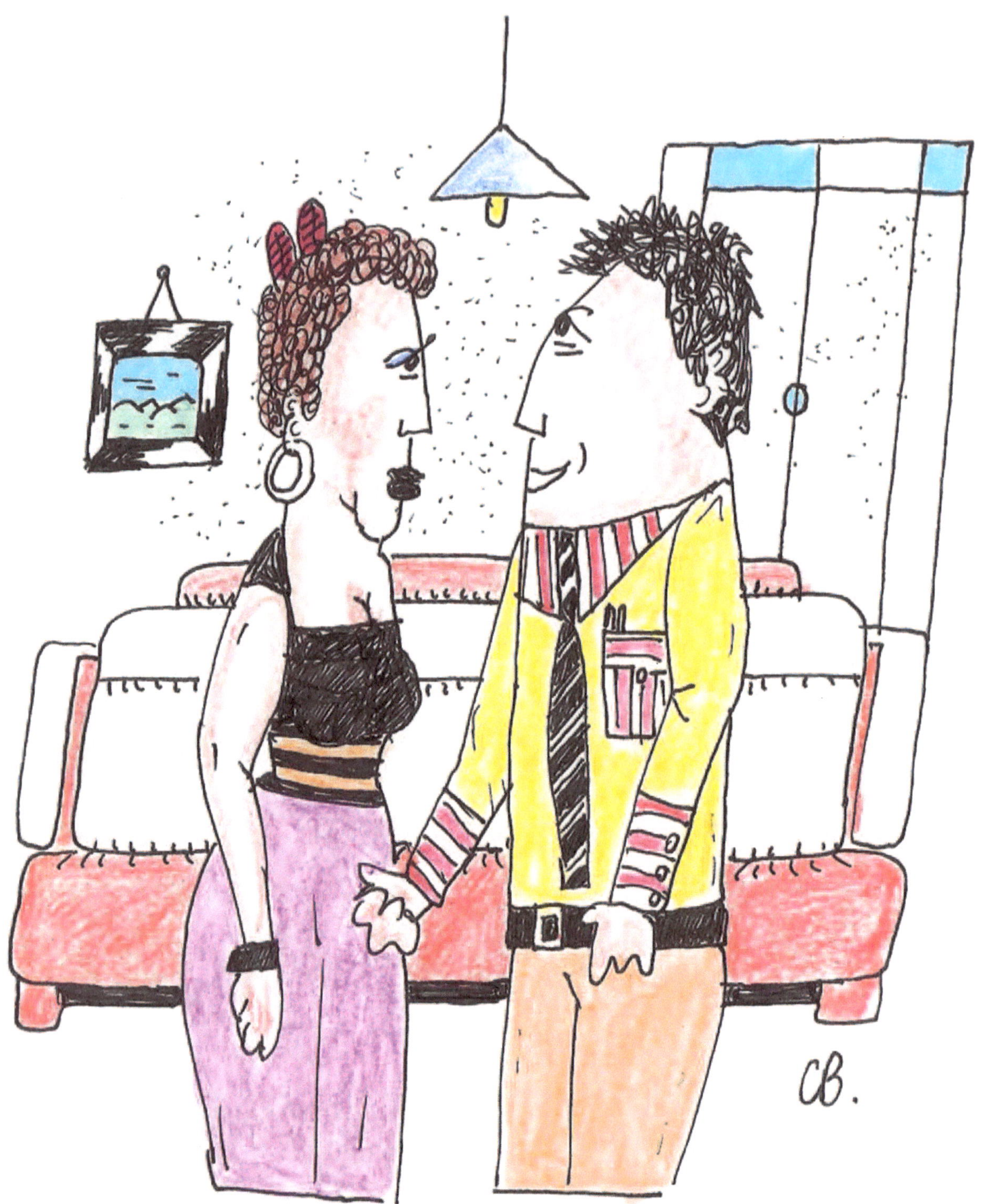

“We need dirtier air...I like to see my air!”

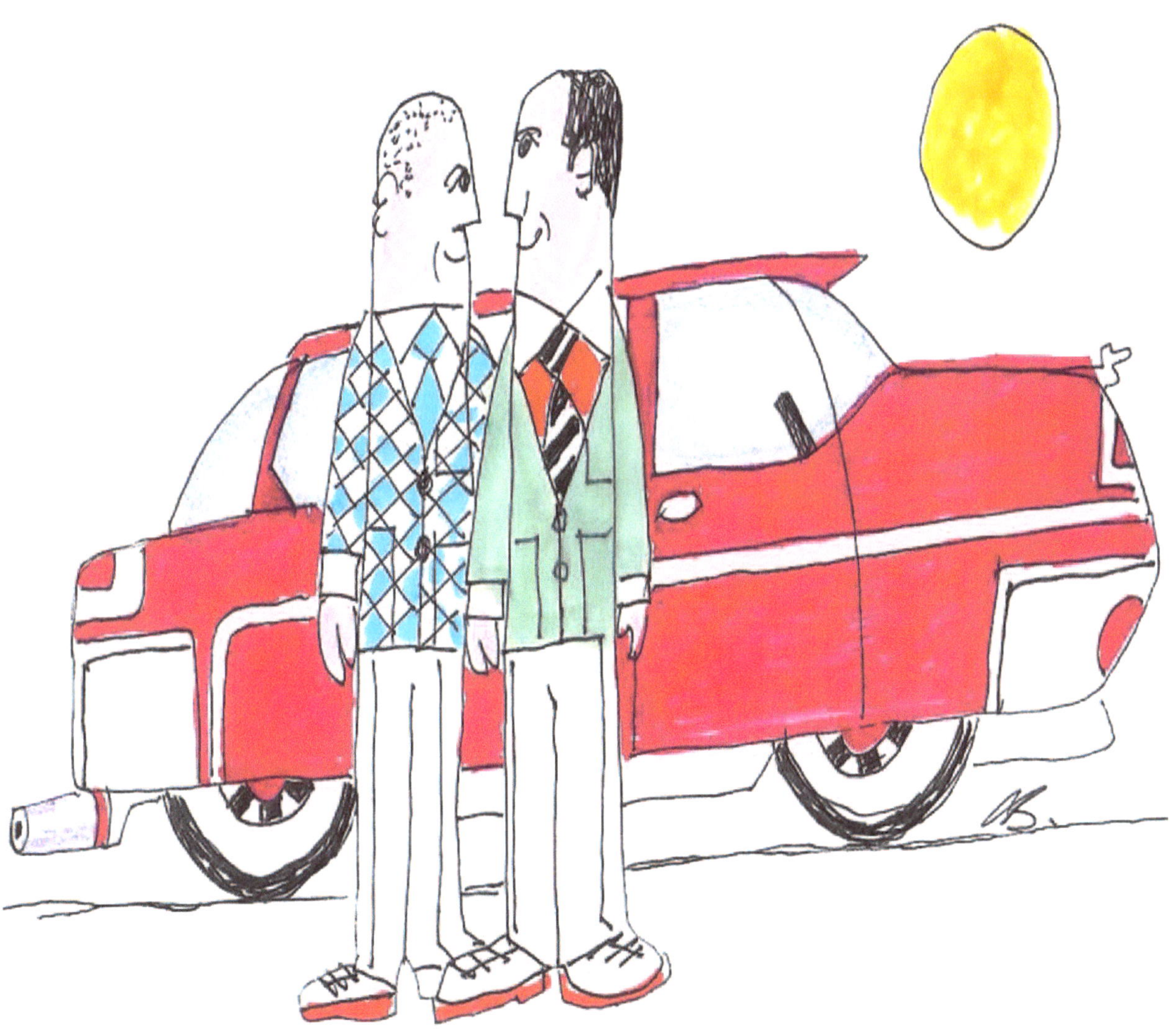

“Finally, a stealth Gas Guzzler designed as a Hybrid.”

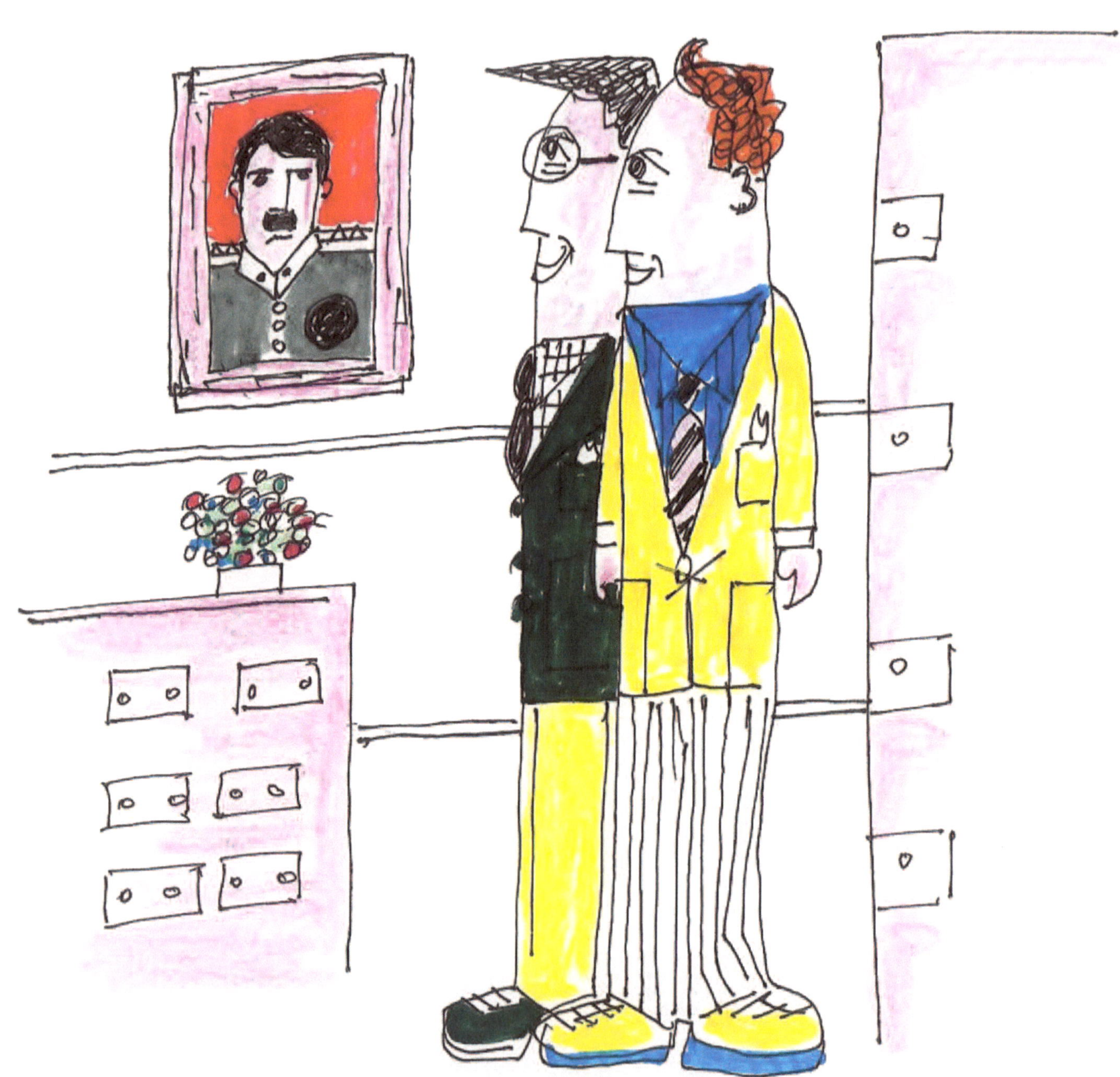

"Does the new Wal-Mart boss look familiar?"

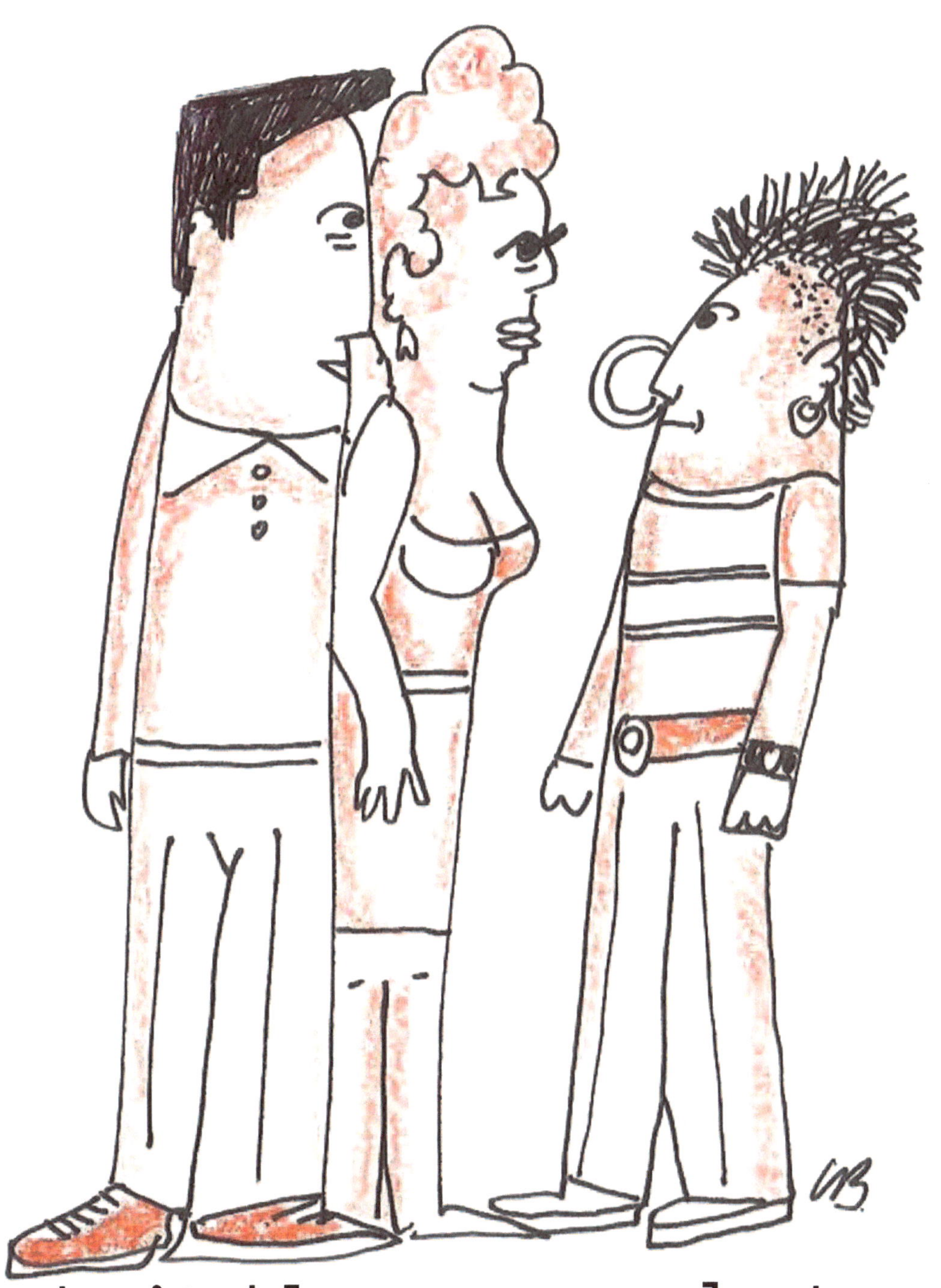

"So don't blame us you lost your sense of smell!"

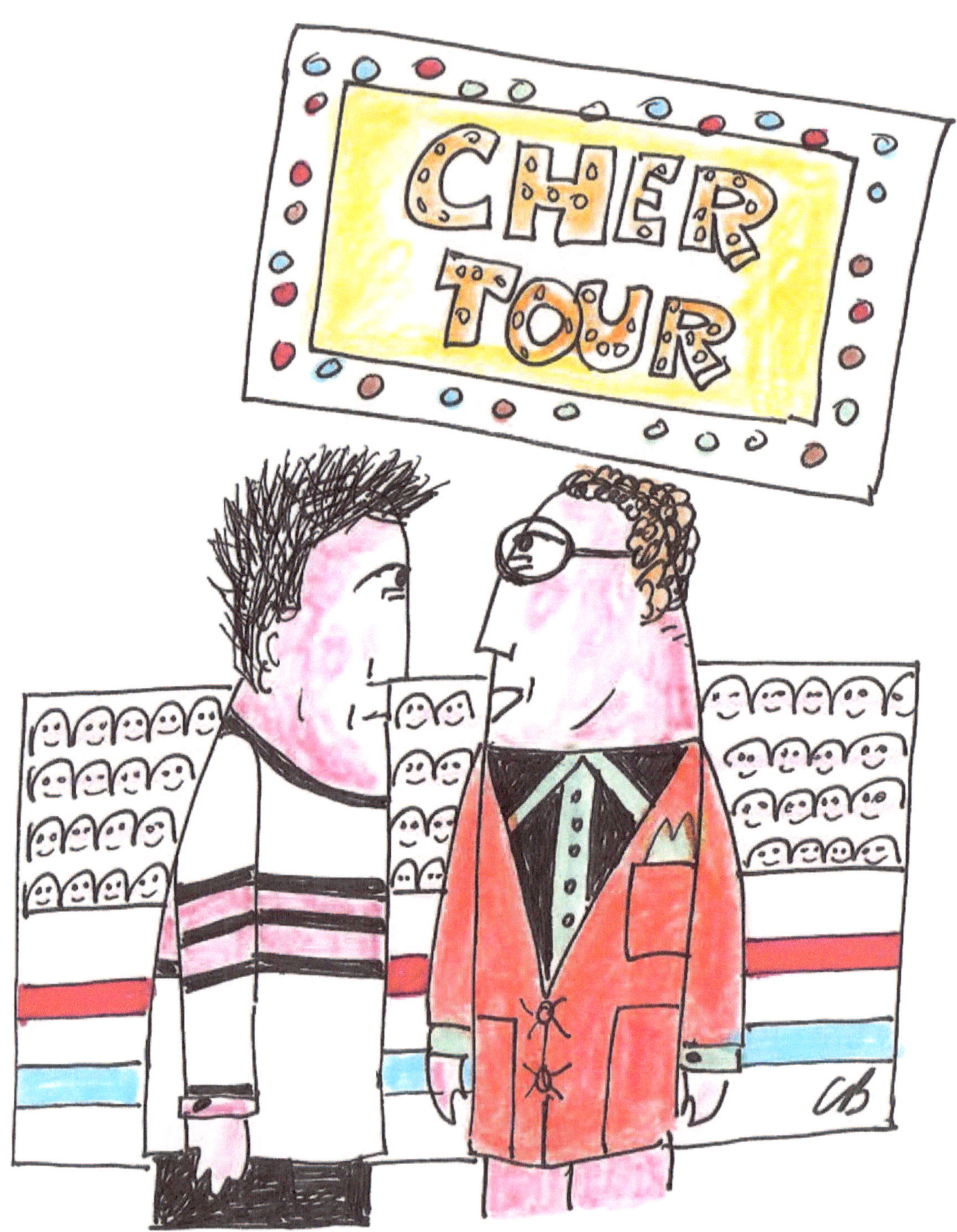

“Don’t ever introduce her as an ”Oldie but Goodie!”

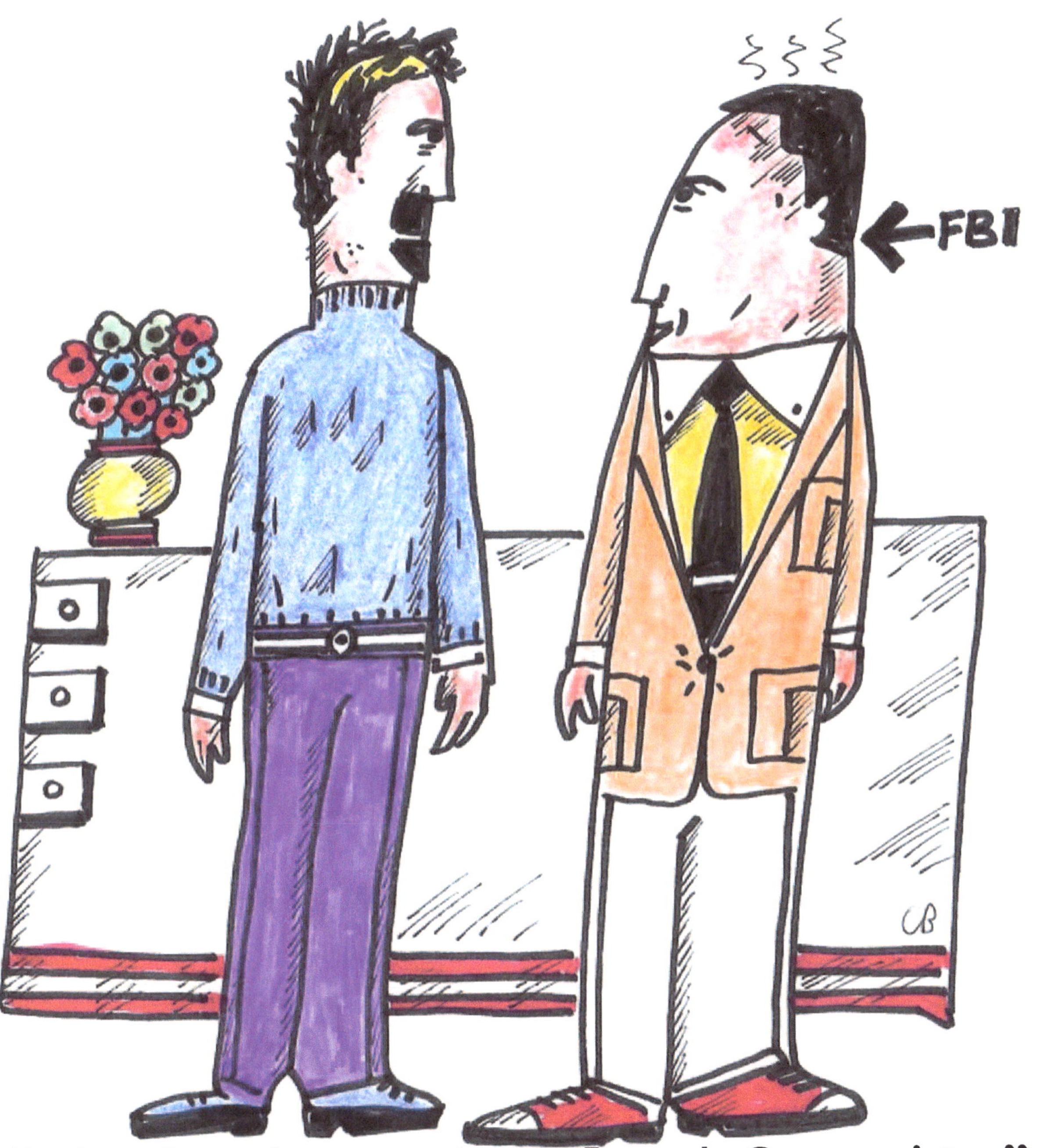

"I'm having a Homeland Security moment."

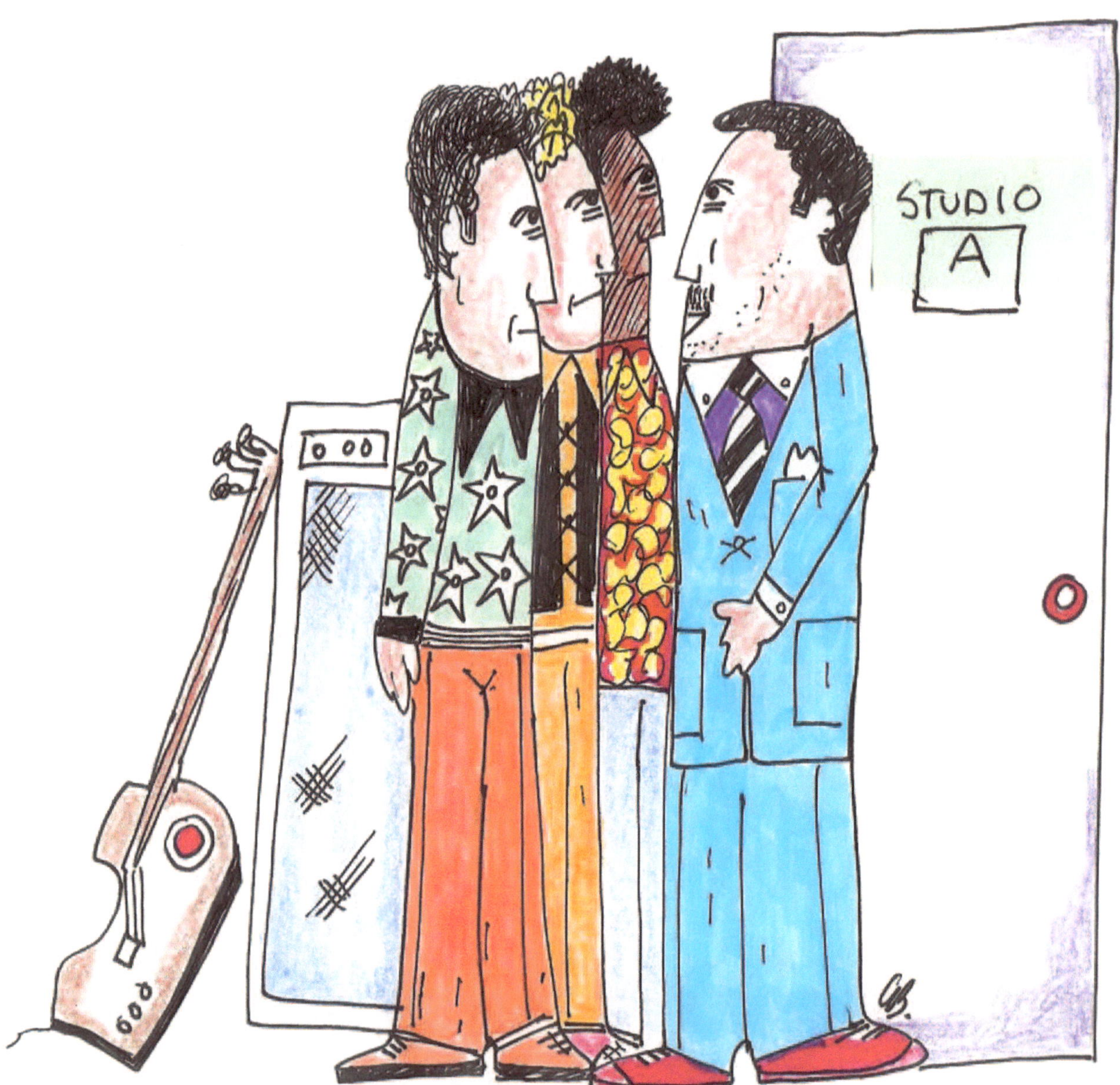

"We need a better name for the band than "Colonoscopy."

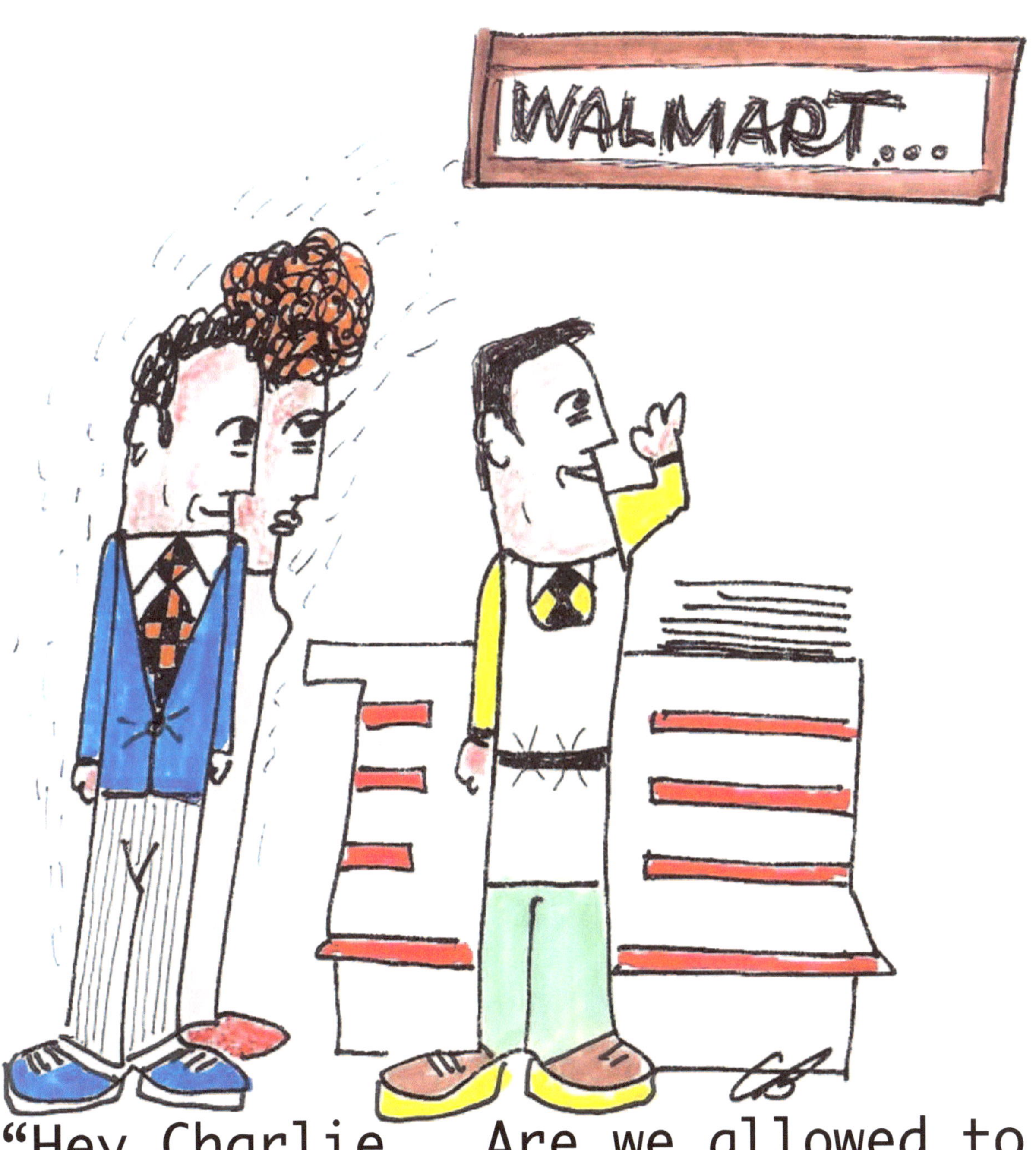

"Hey Charlie...Are we allowed to sell American flags to Liberals?"

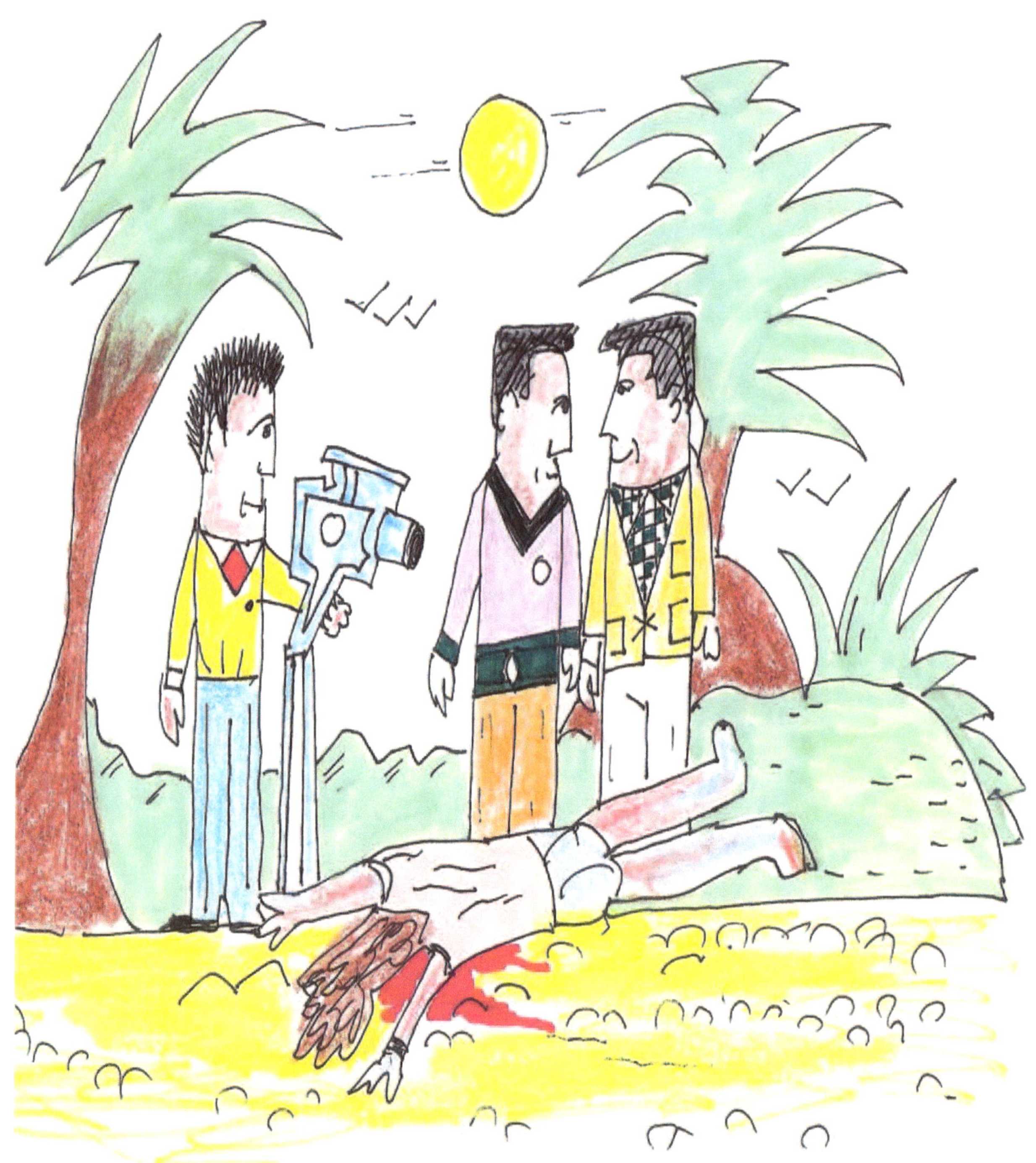

“Carl, the idea of ”Survivor“, is the winner has to live!!”

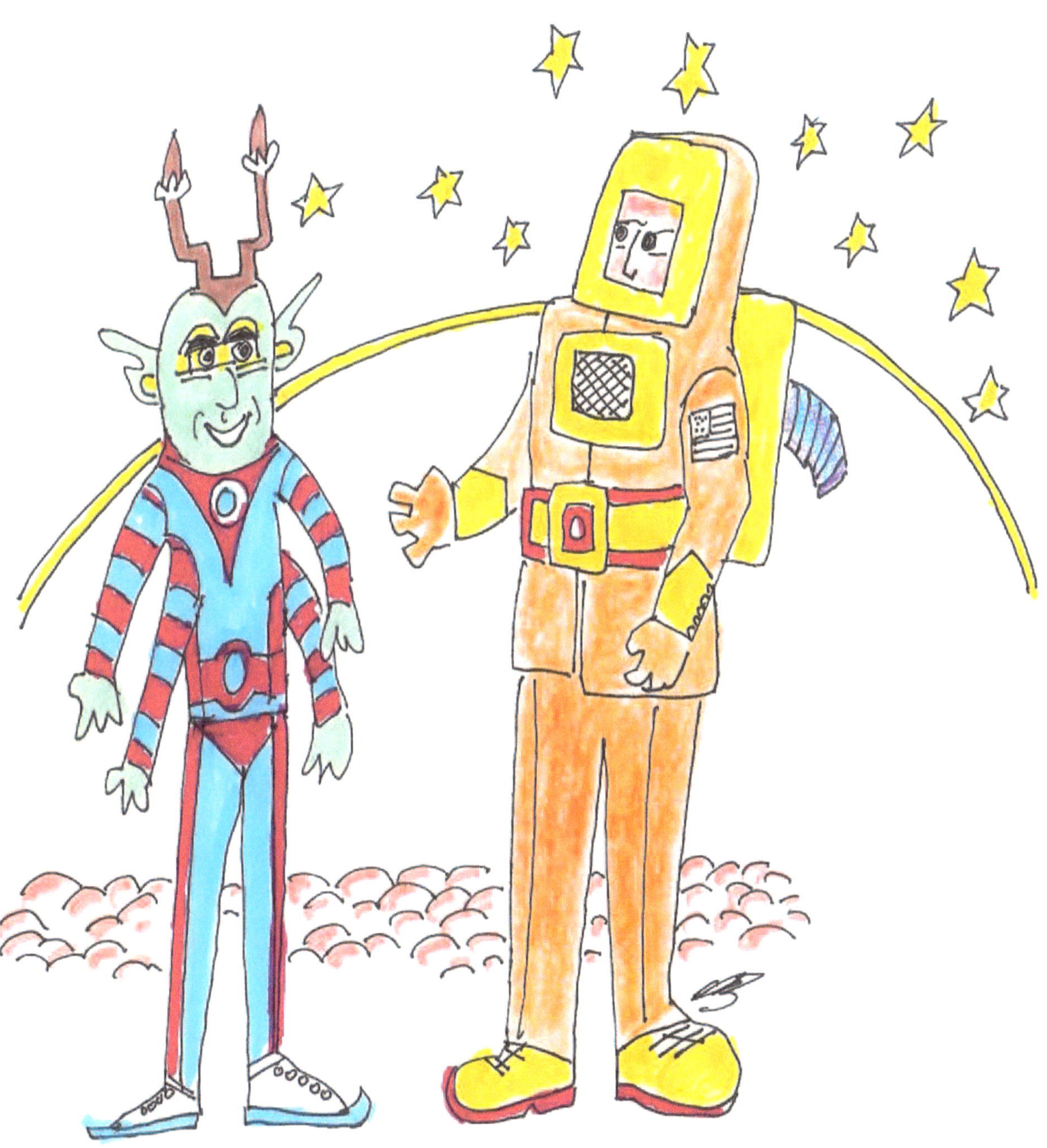

"Take me to your manicurists."

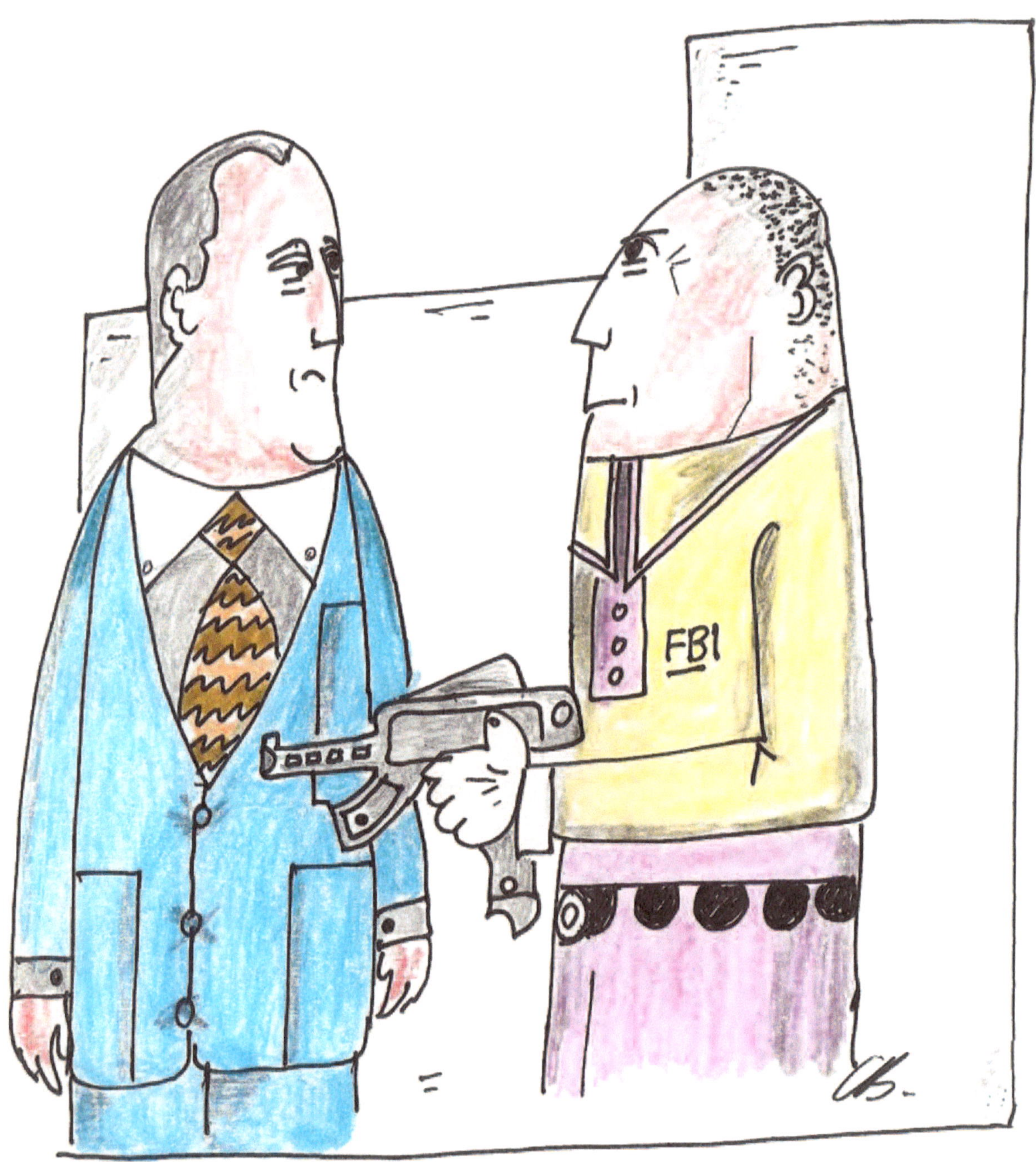

"You're under arrest for not believing in our version of a just God!"

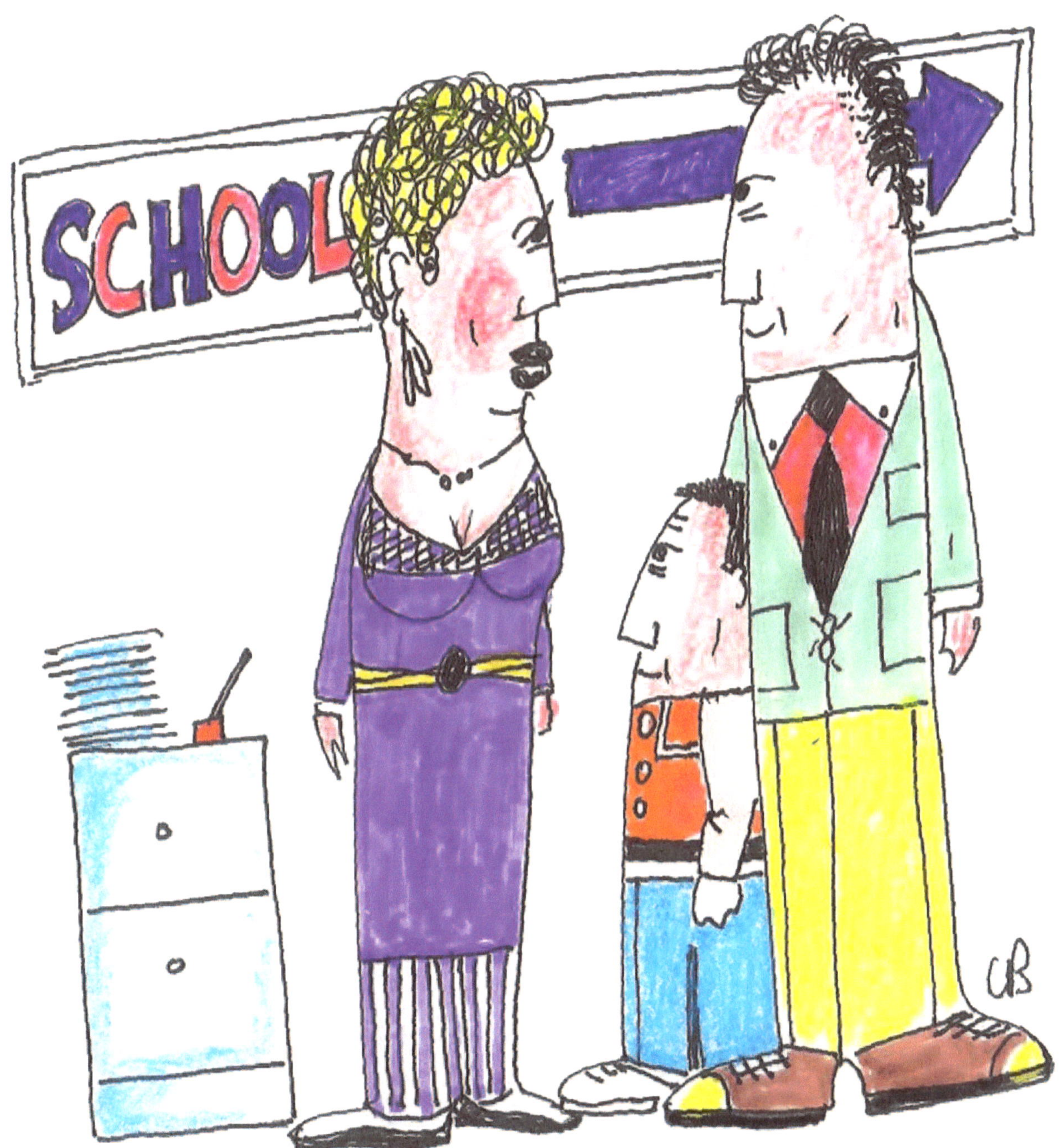

"Mervin is an almost illiterate kid with a racist chip. He's well on his way to a Tea Party career."

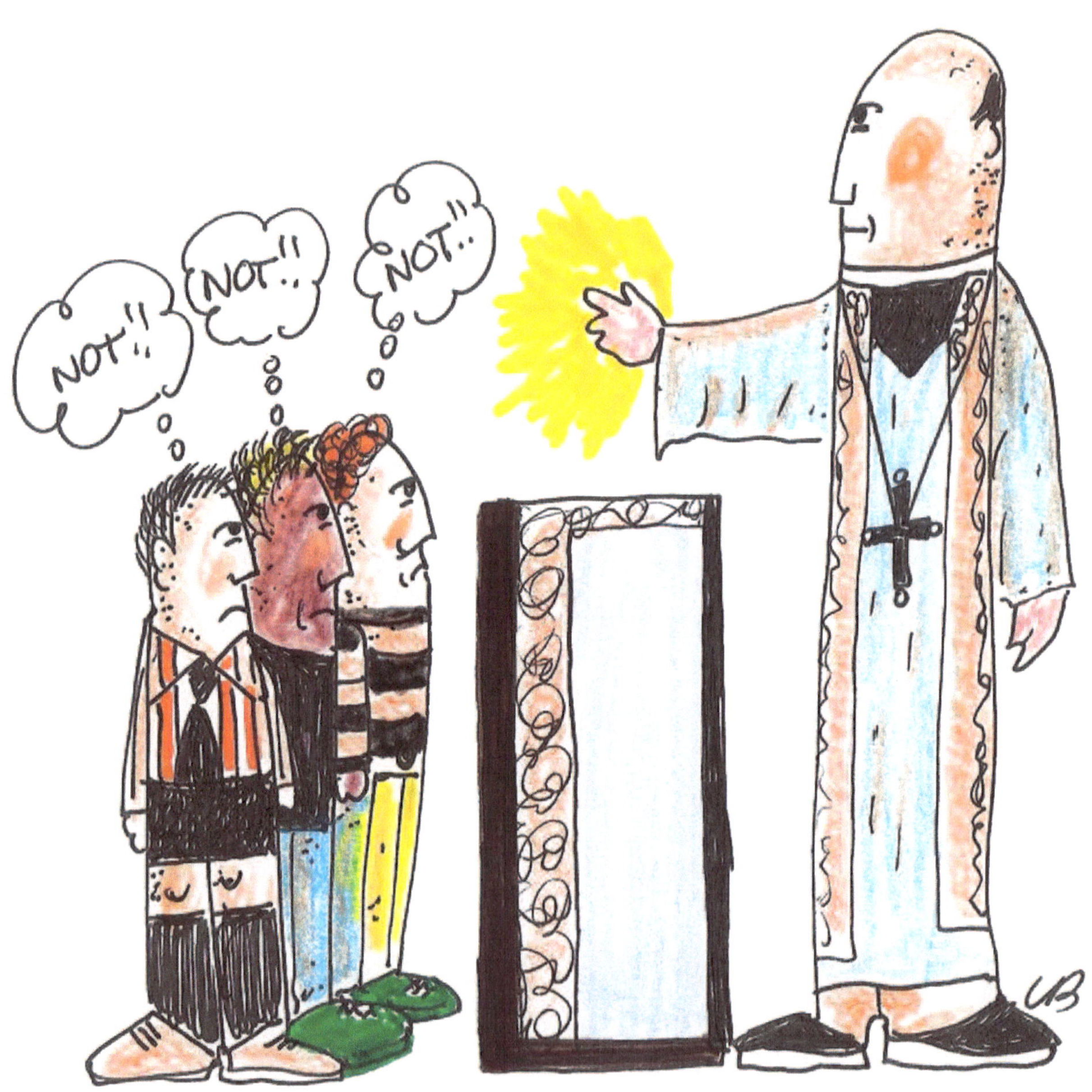
NOT!!
NOT!!
NOT!!

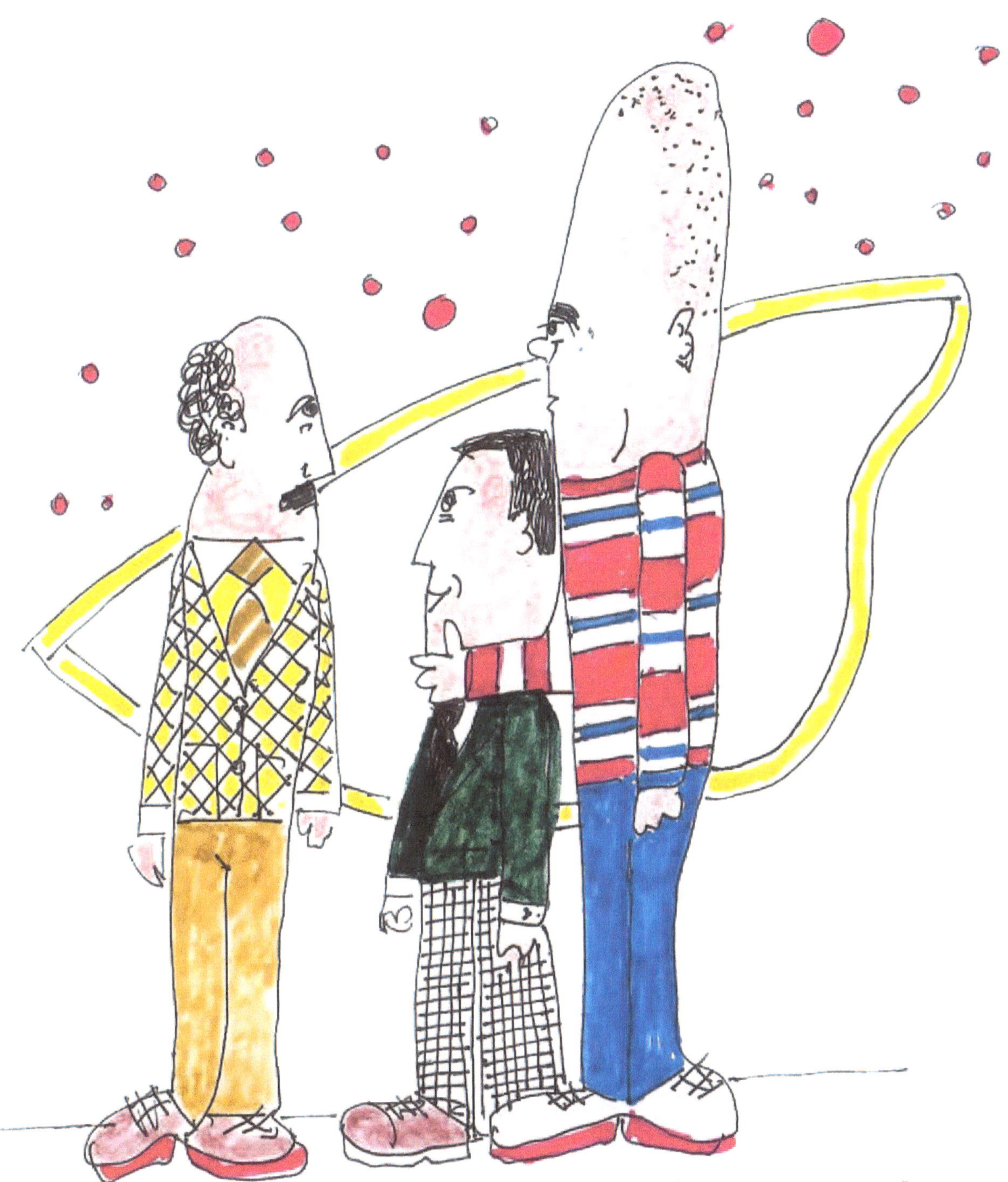

“This is Otto. He invented everything there is so far this century.”

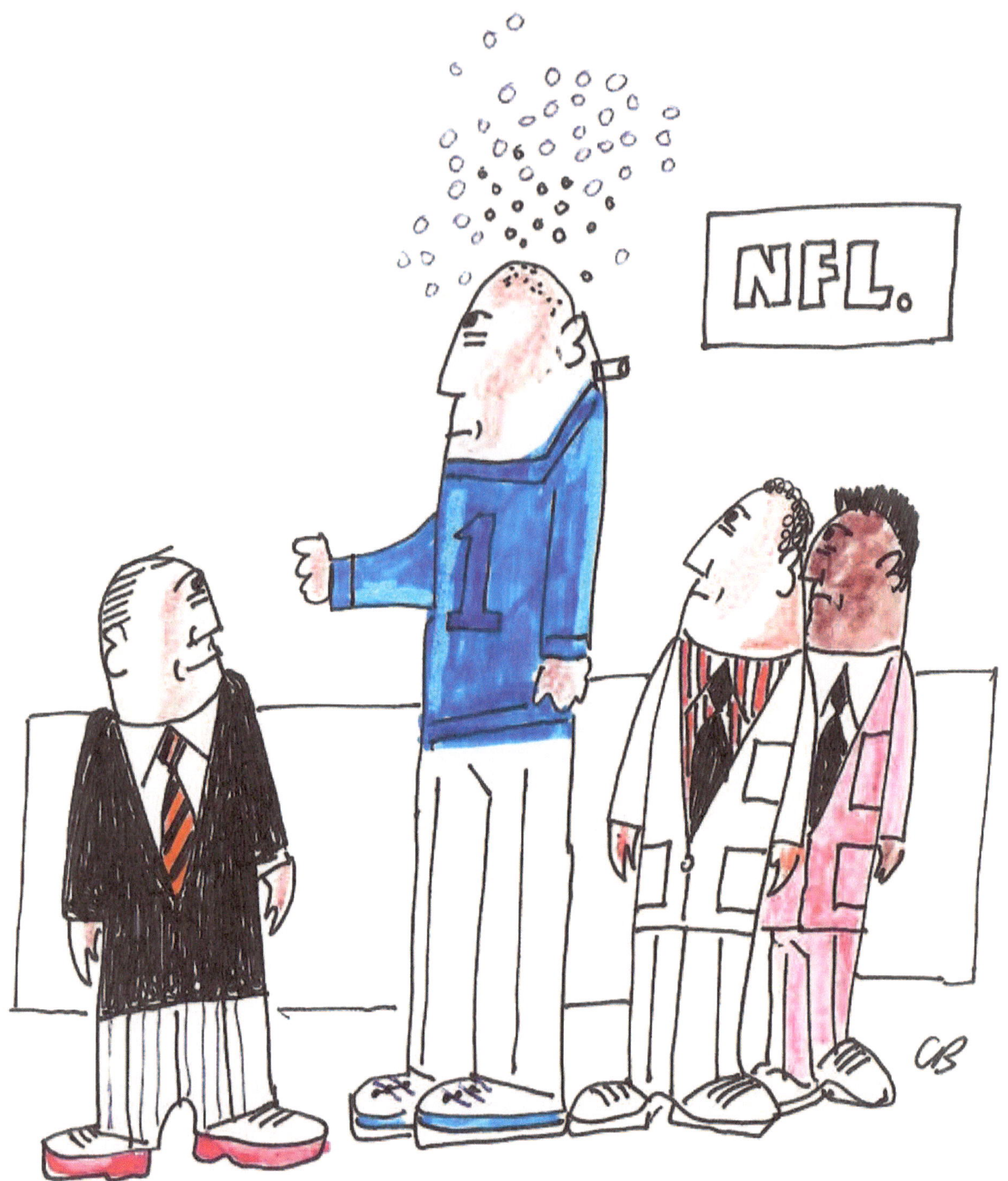

"This is the first of the cloned Line Backers. He's completely made of life like Teflon."

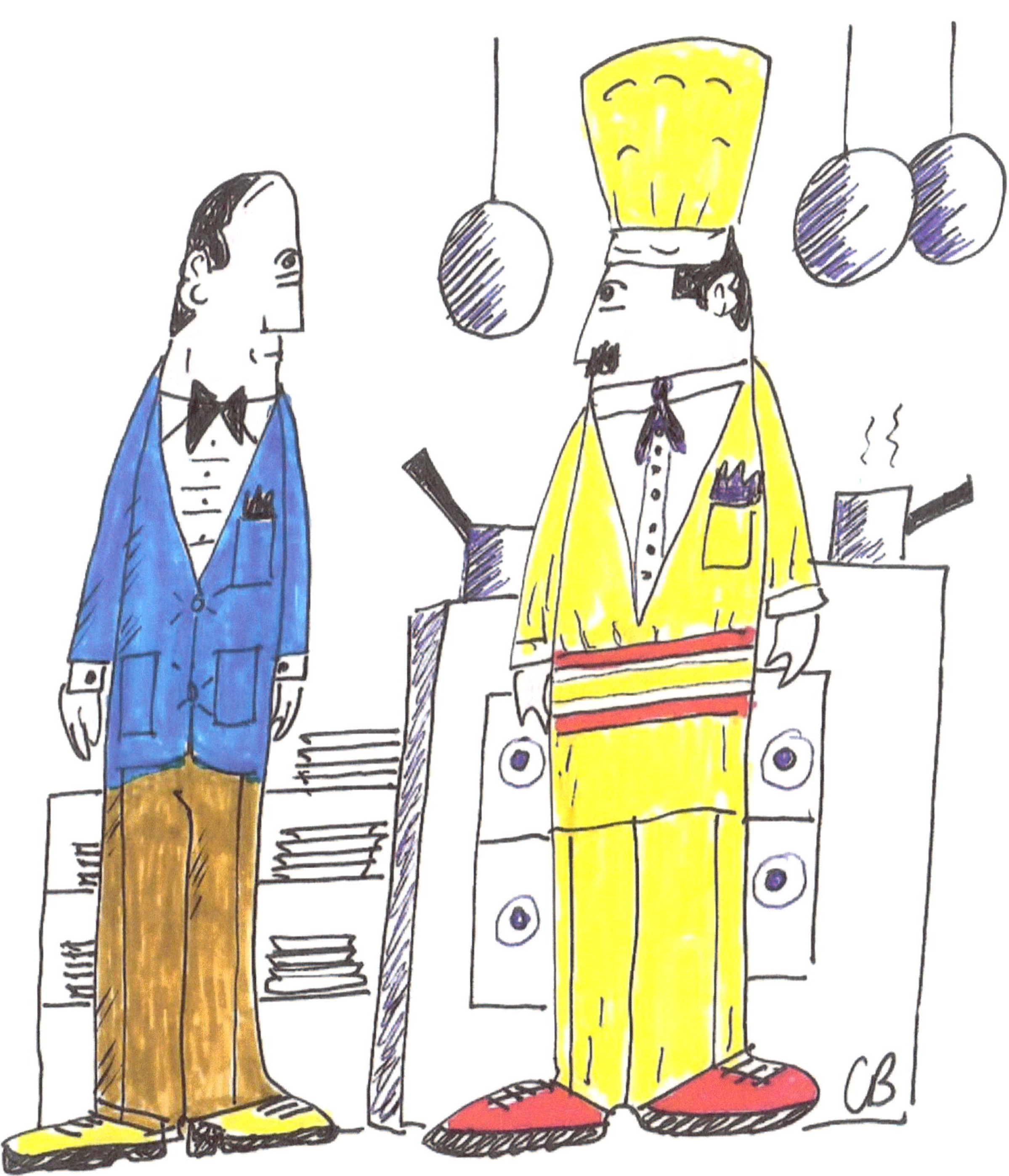

"My souffle just had a problem that even Dr. Phil can't fix."

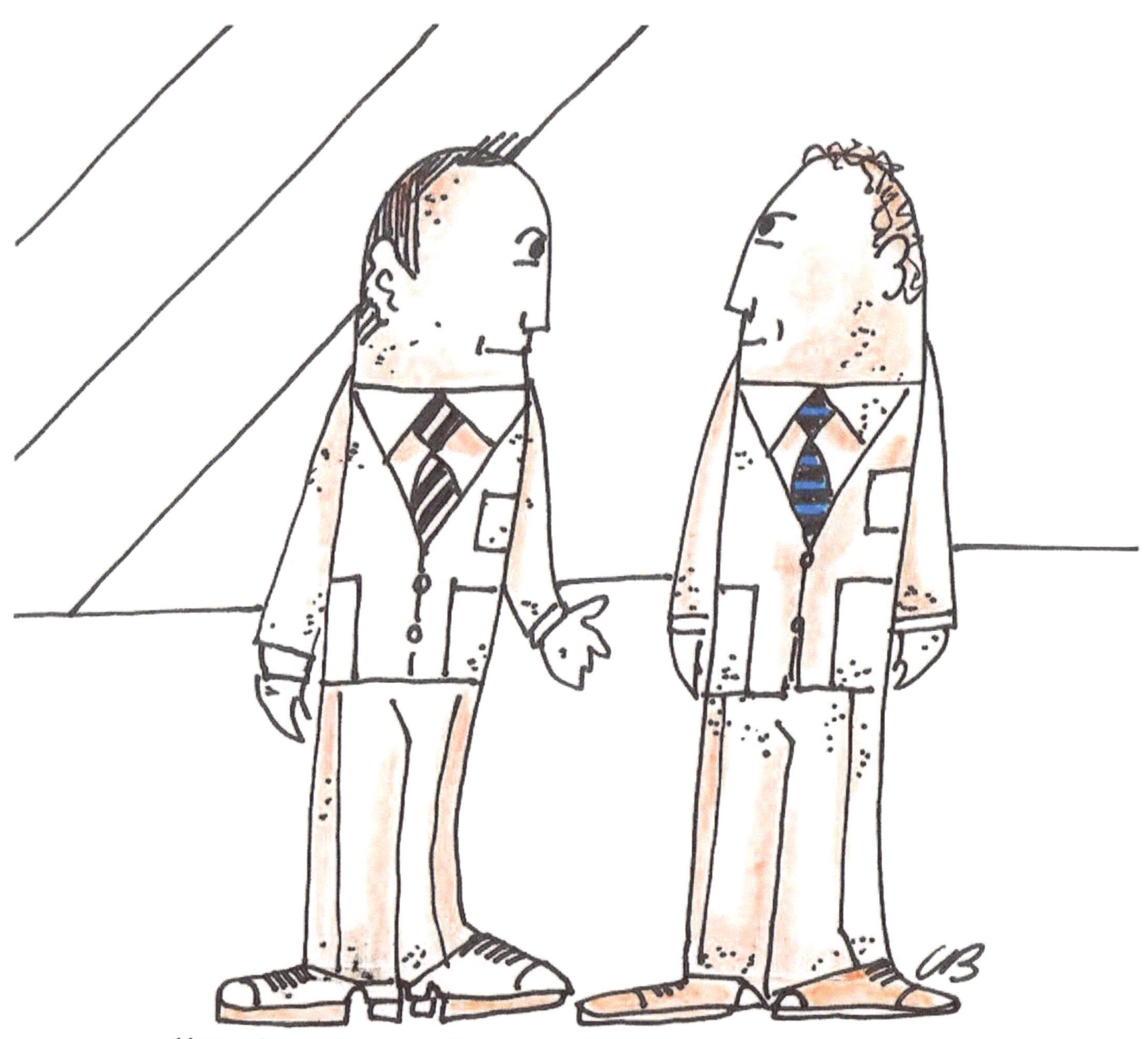

"I had a four hour erection last night. Luckily I was with the Dallas Cheerleaders."

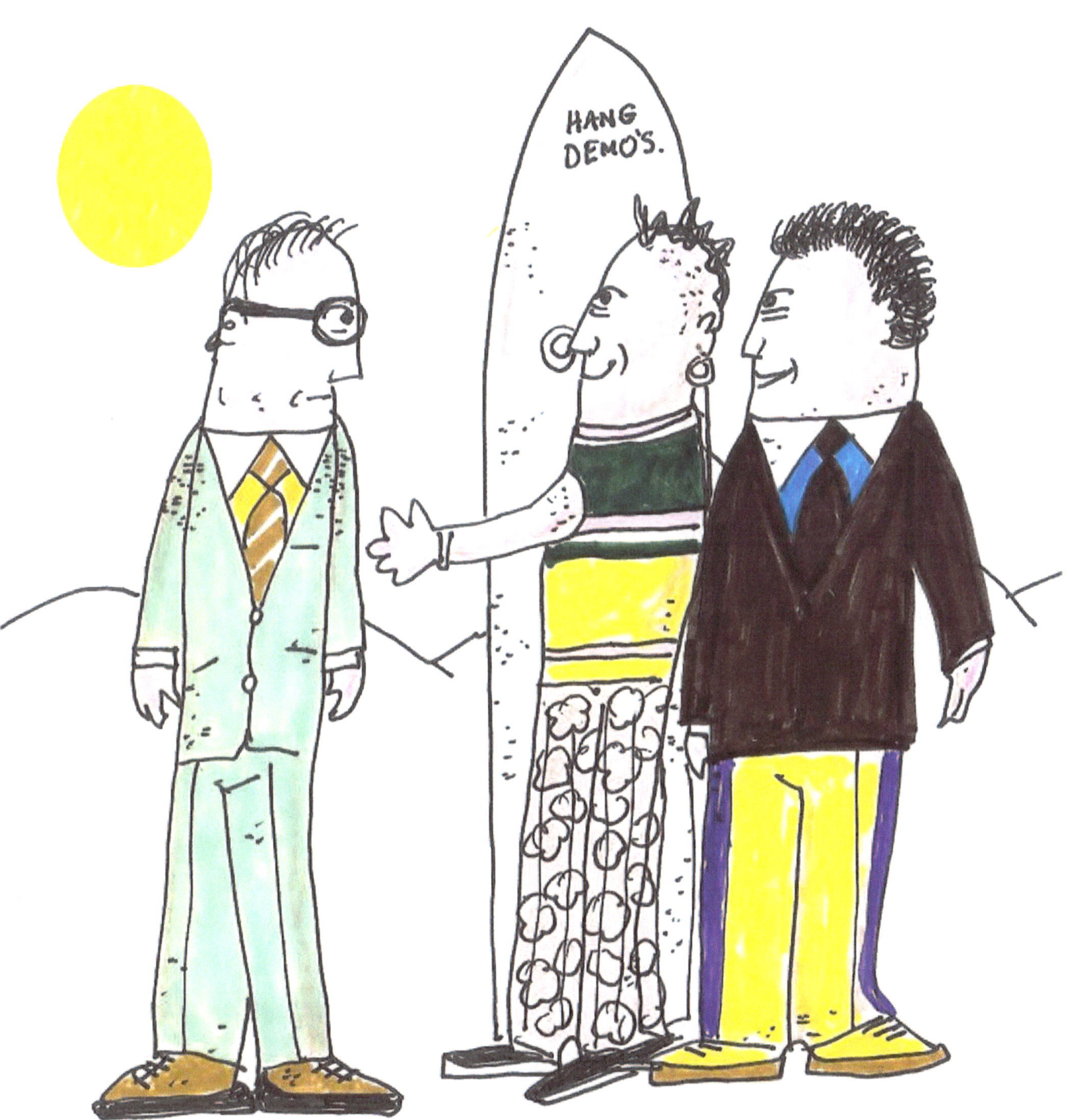

“I found the only Tea Party Surfer in California.”

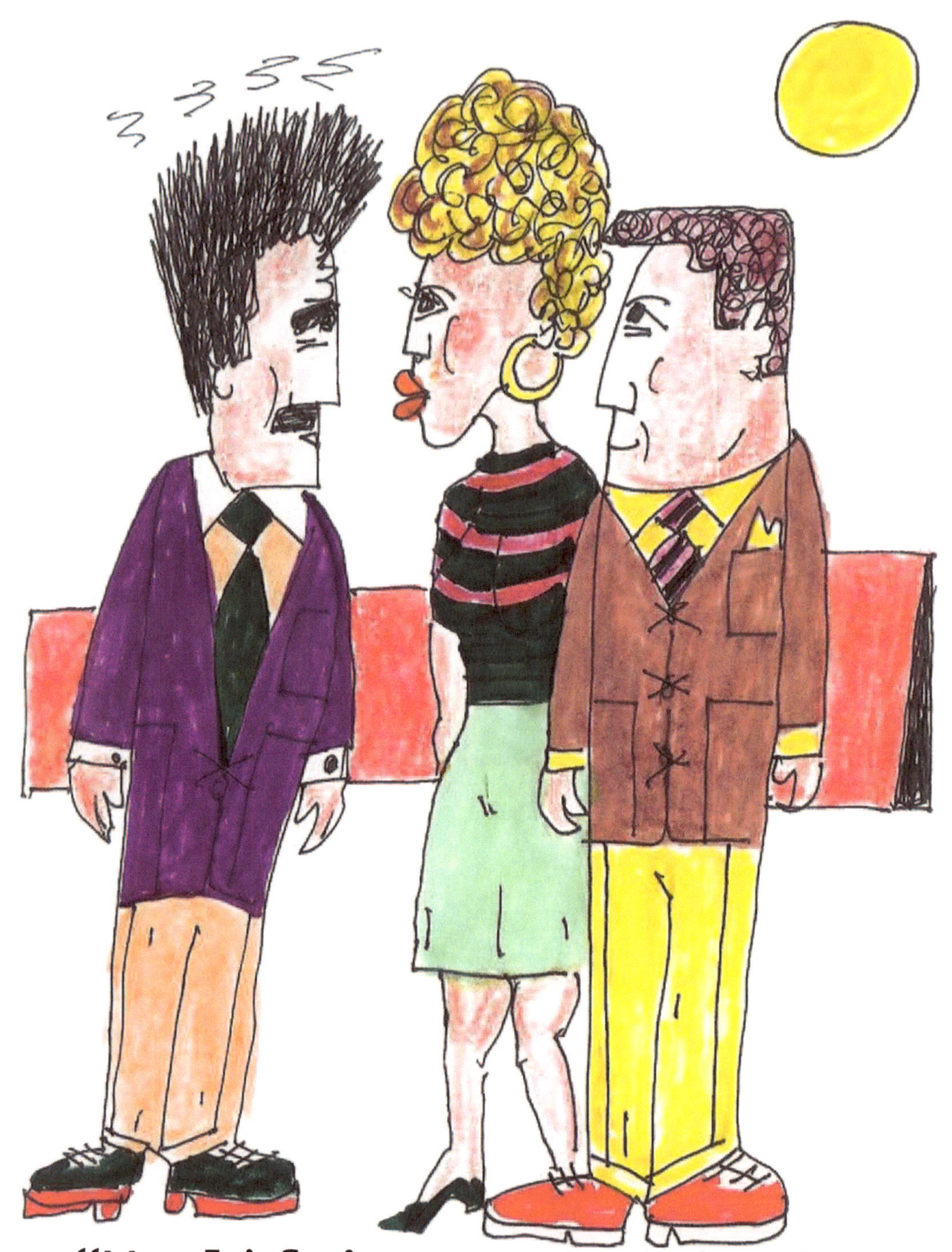

"My life's an open book.
Unfortunately, it's in Polish."

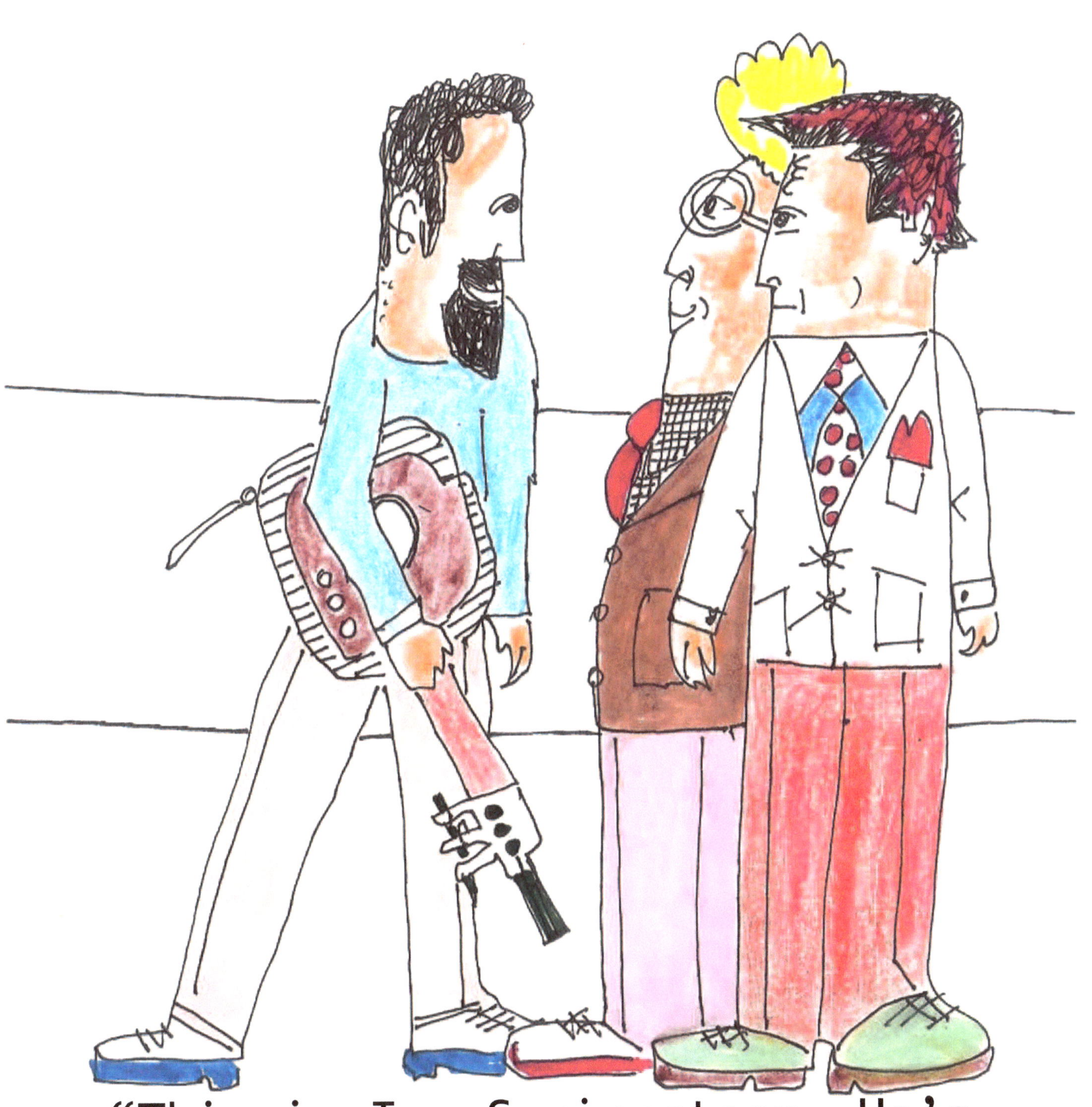

“This is Irv Springsteen. He’s no Bruce...but he works for scale.”

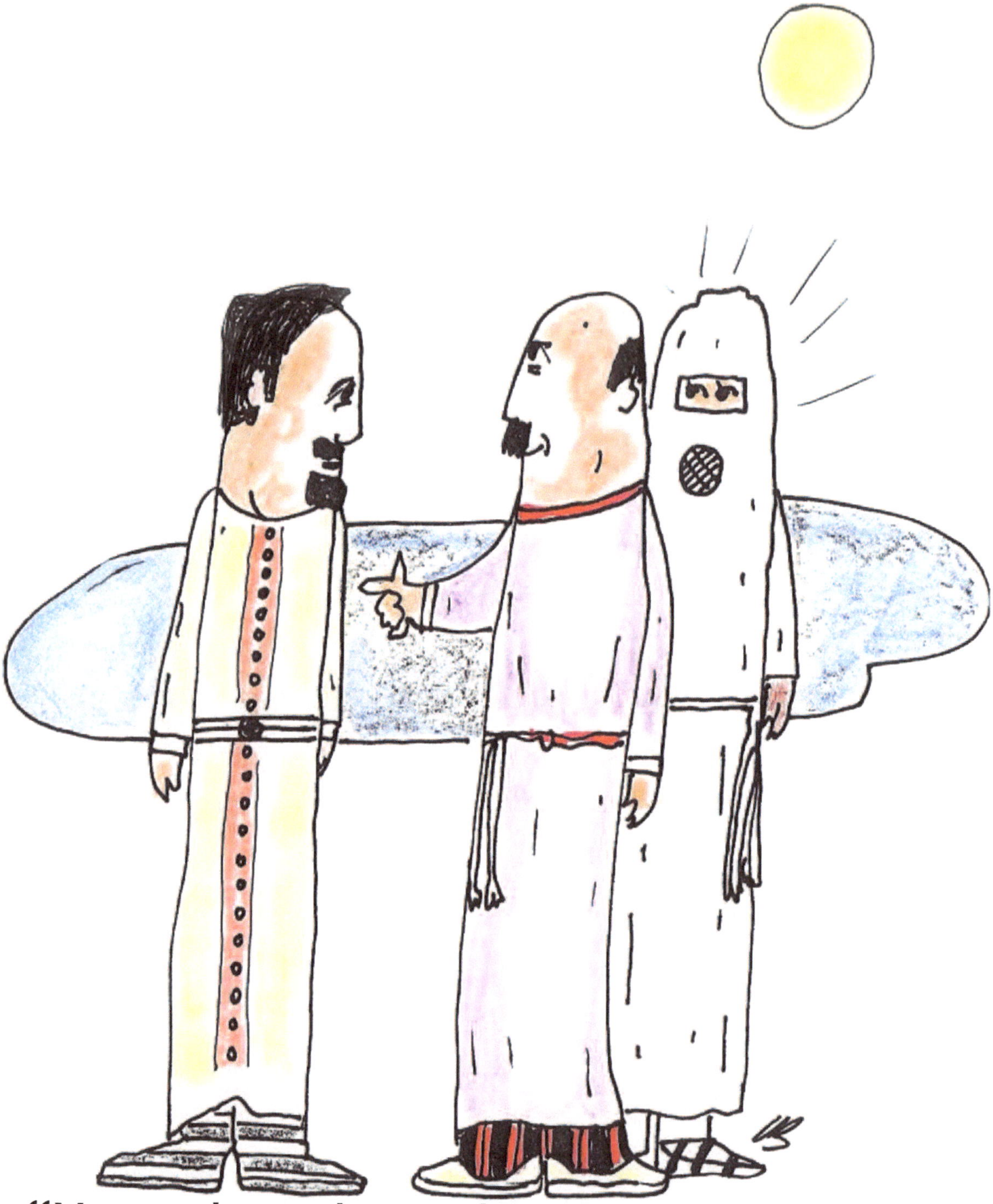

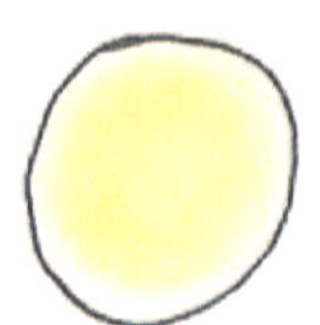

"Yes, but how do you know this isn't Cameron Diaz?"

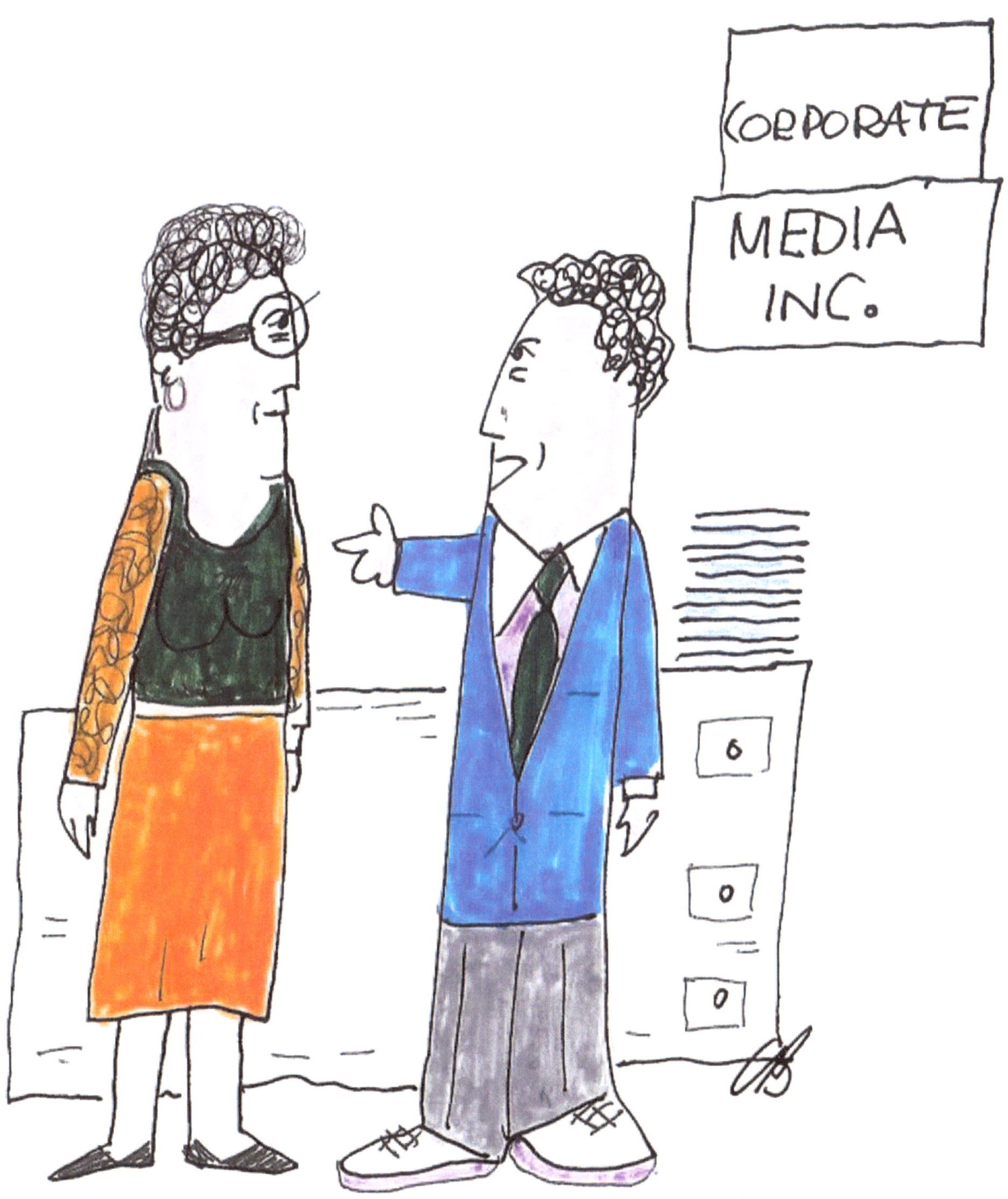

"Sorry Mavis, you're outsourced."

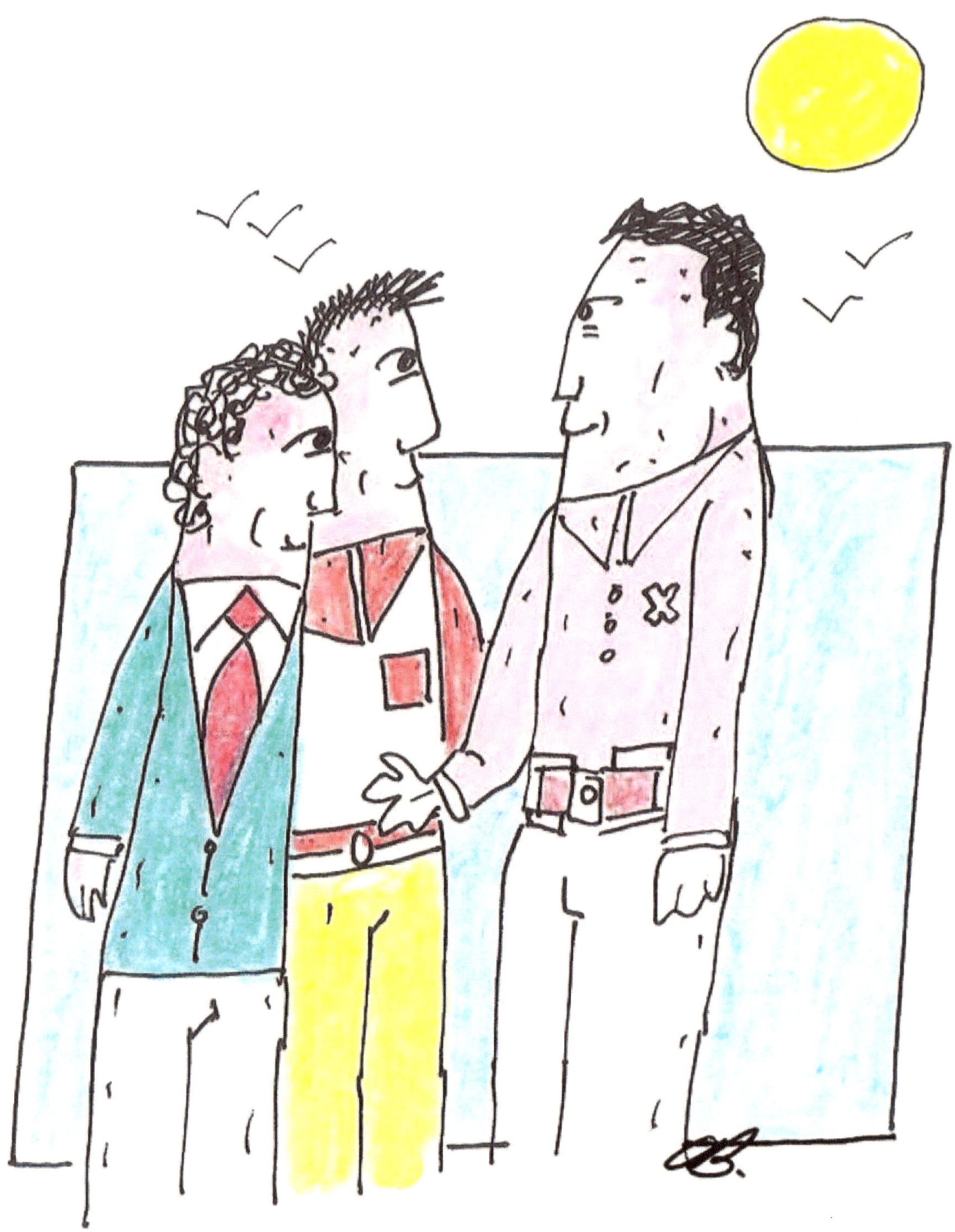

"My wife left me for another loser."

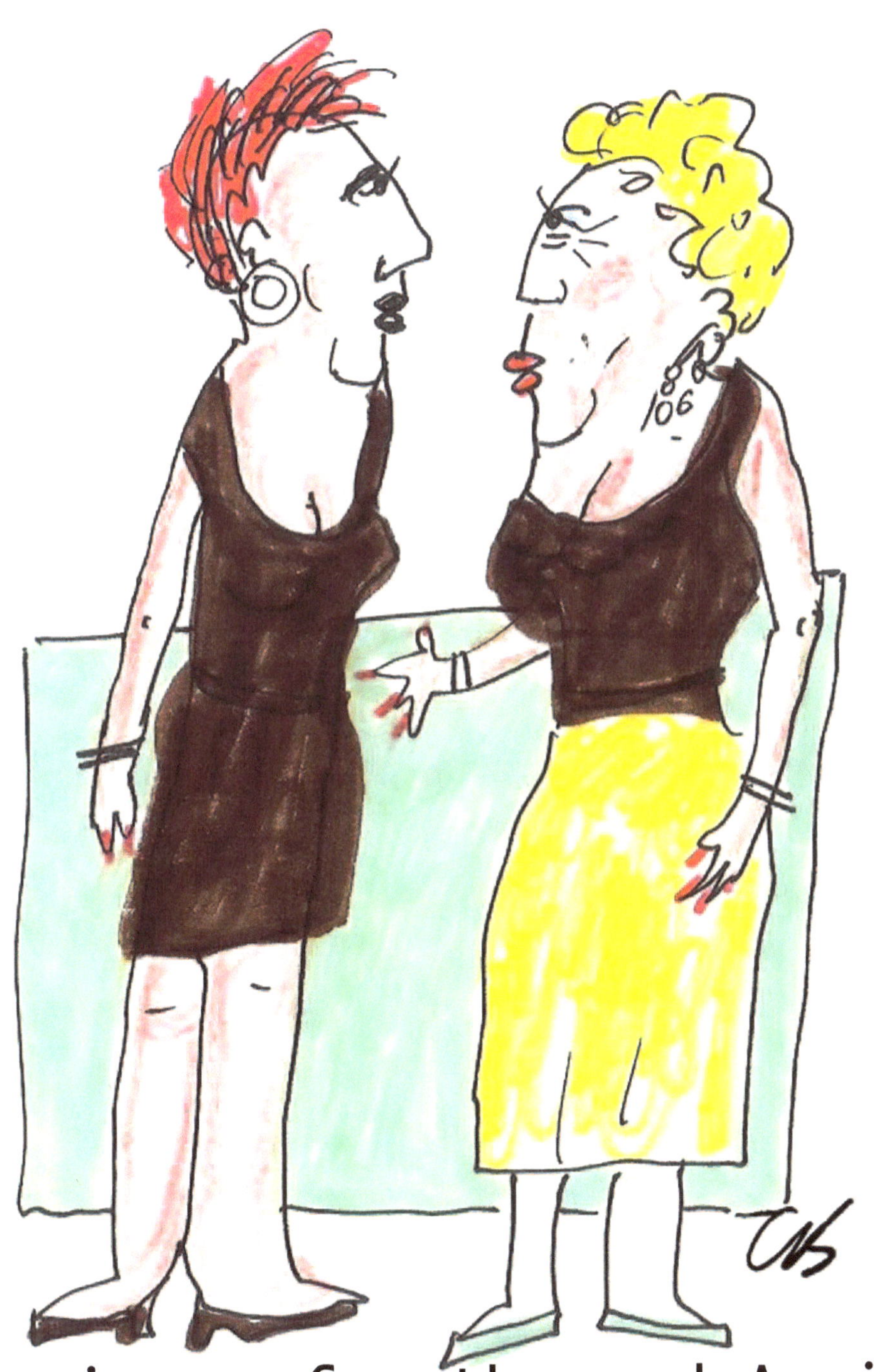

"This is my fourth, and Arnie's fifth marriage...We're planning a gray wedding."

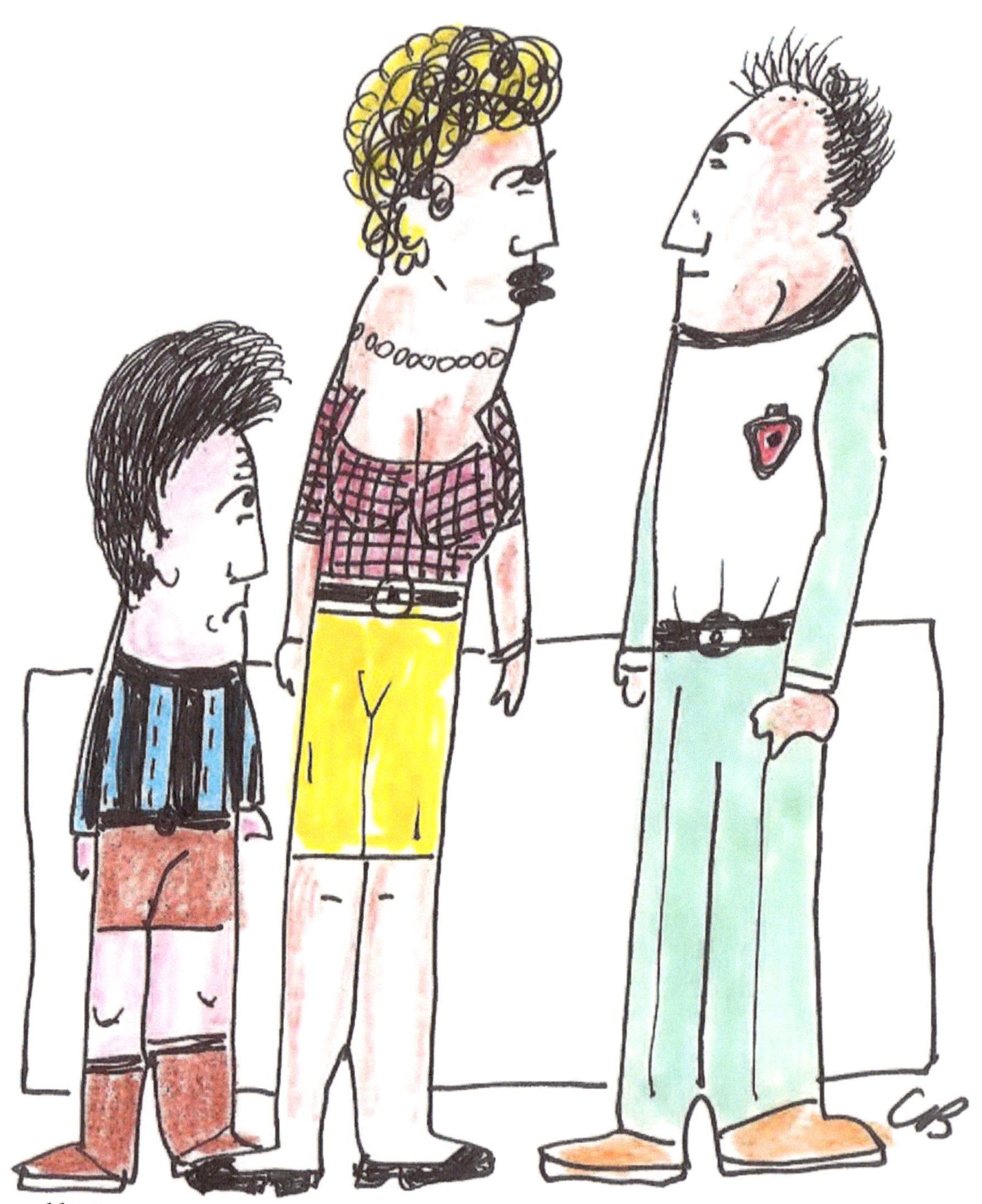

"Your son wants to join the Madding crowd."

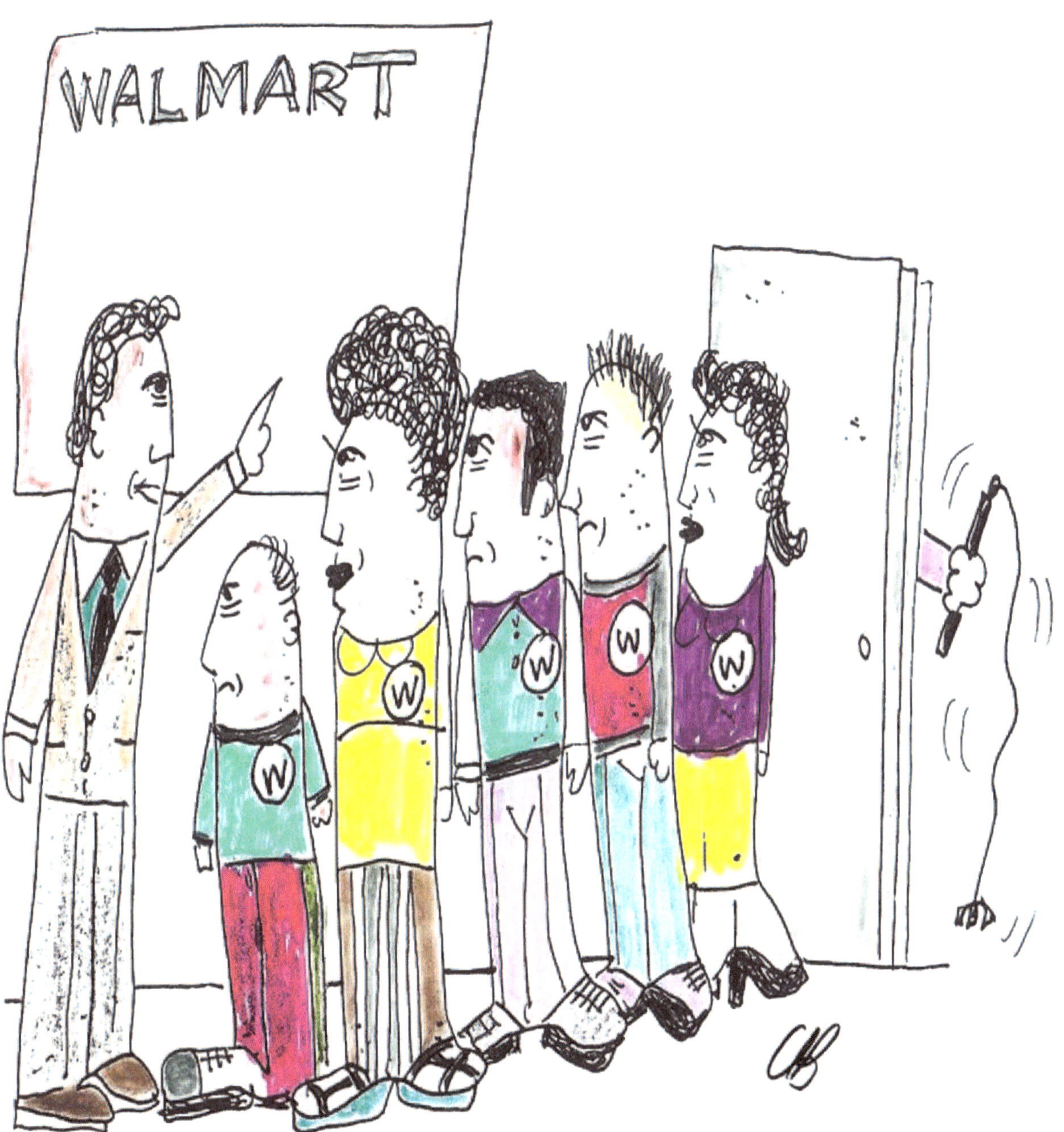

"First one to yell "LUNCH", gets the Cat-O-Nine Tails!"

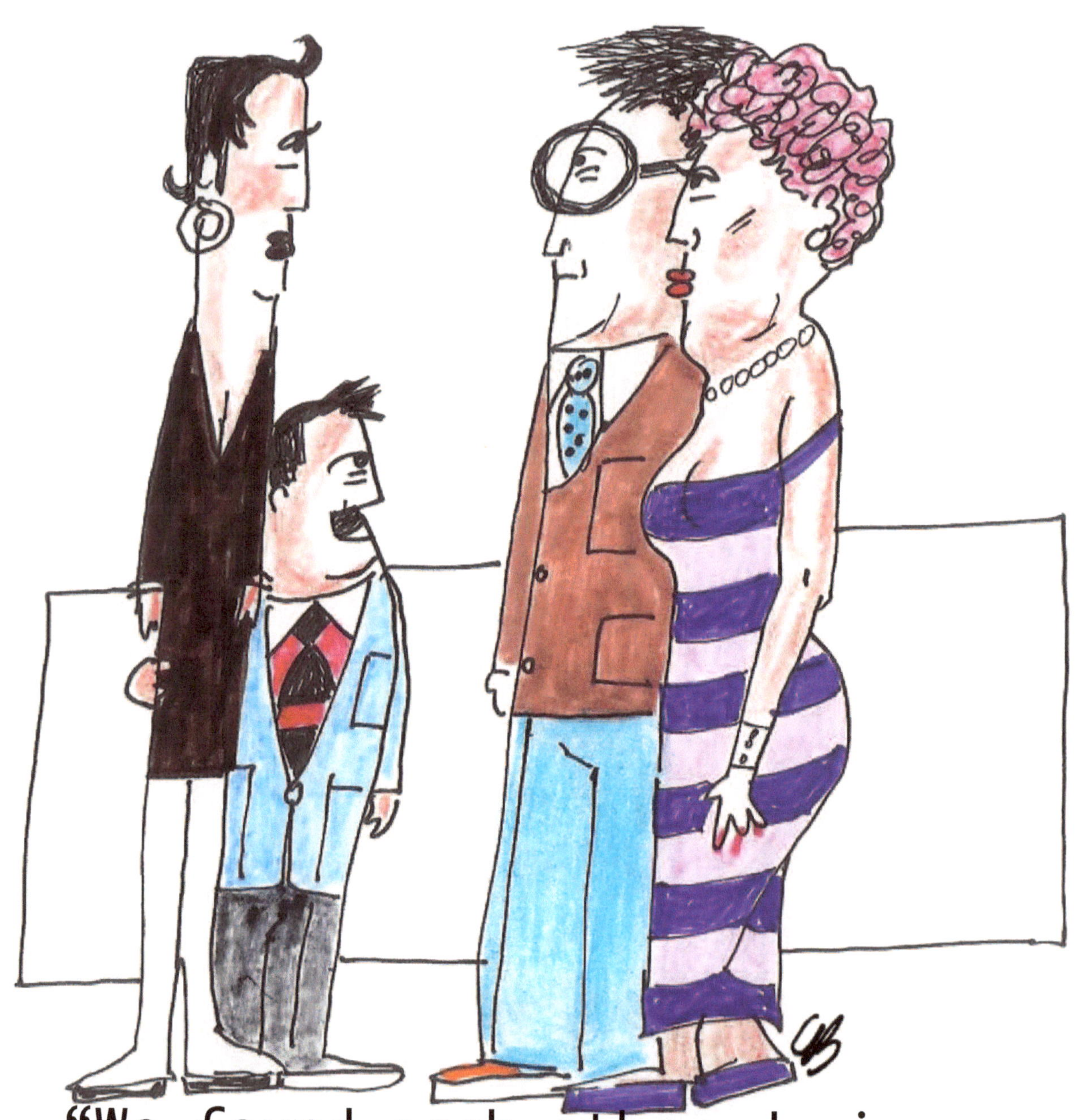

"We found each other during a computer dating glitch."

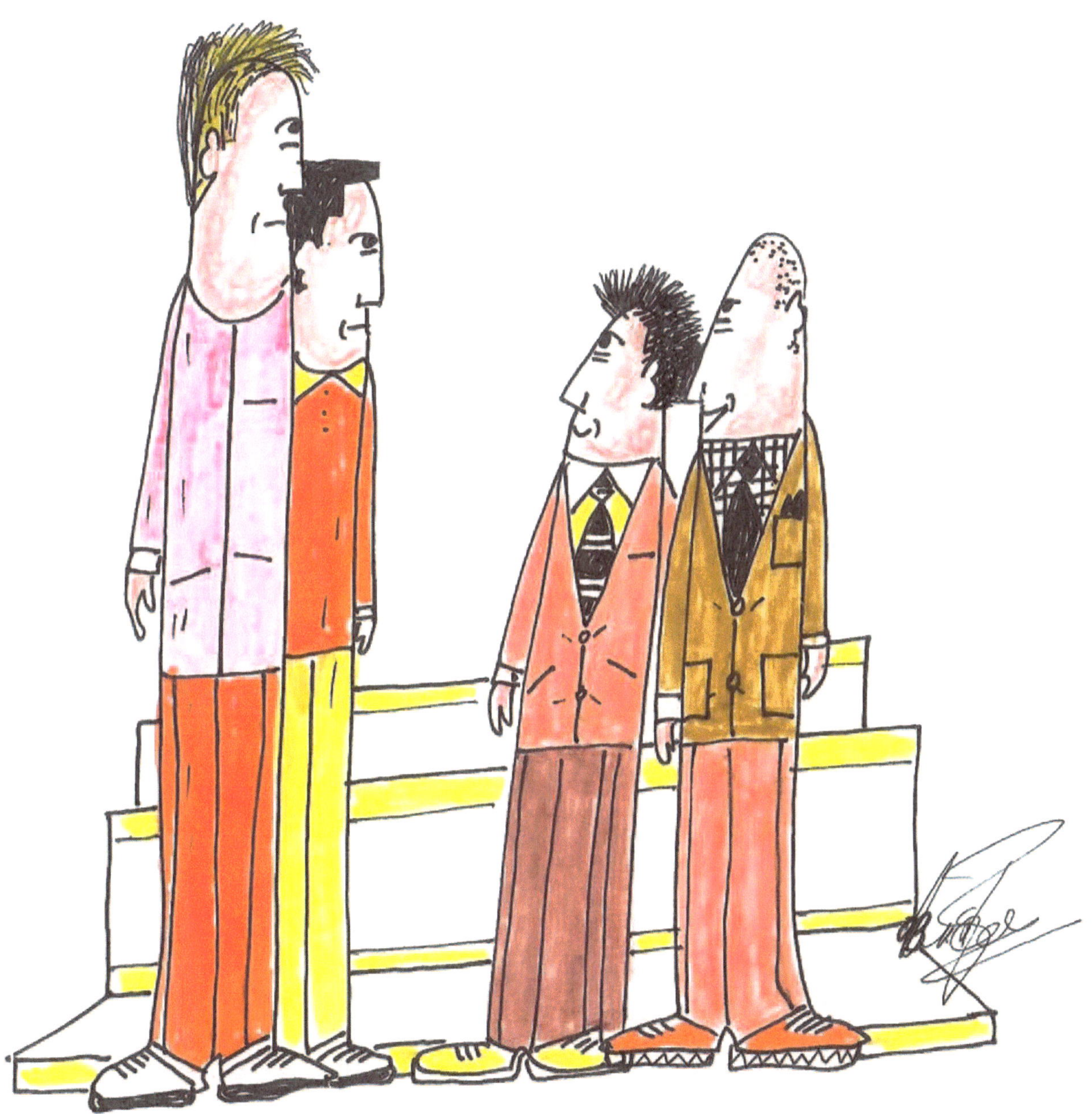

“Serbia’s finest hoop stars & fortunately, reformed war criminals.”

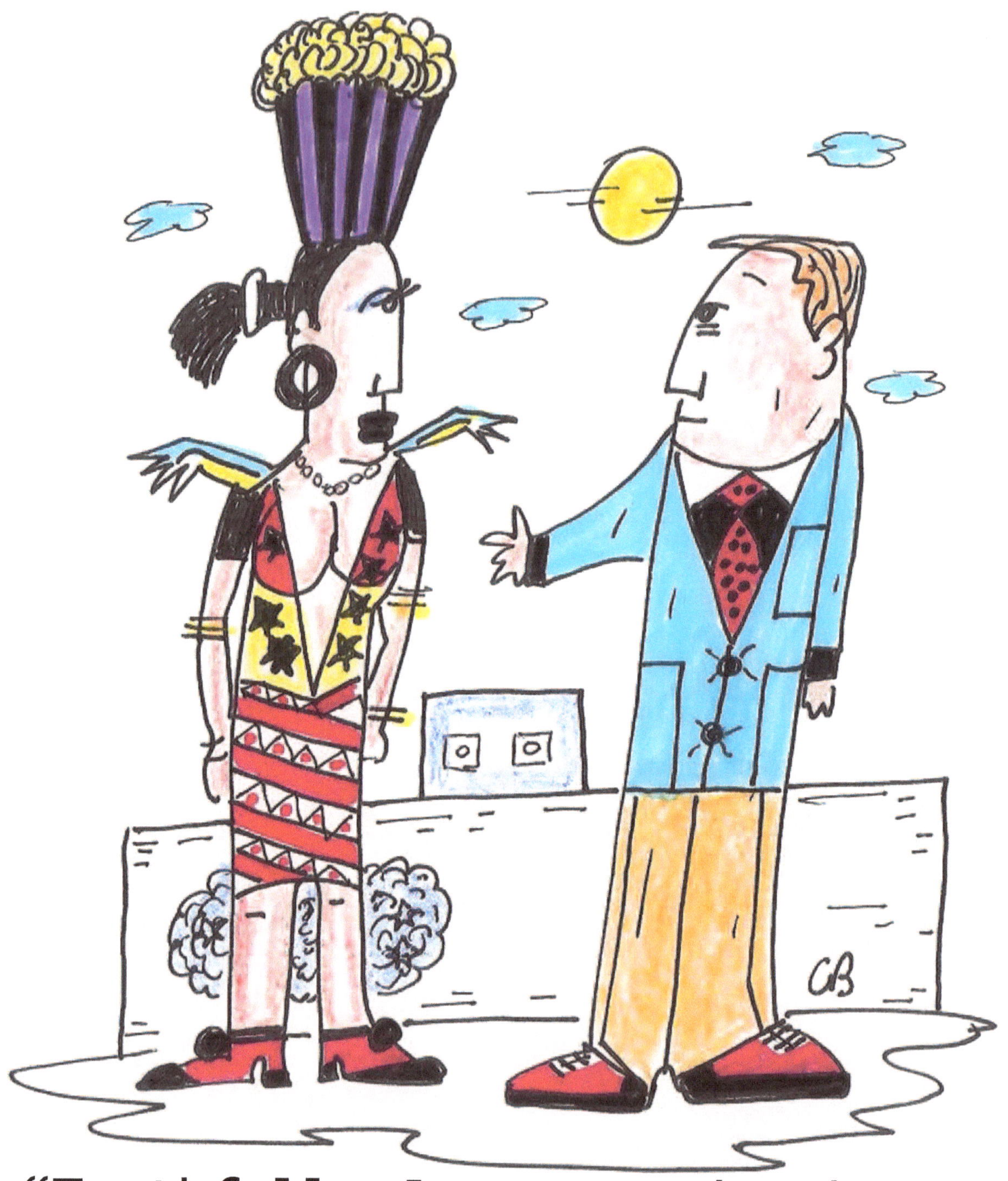

"Truthfully Joanne...the dress looked better on Lady GaGa."

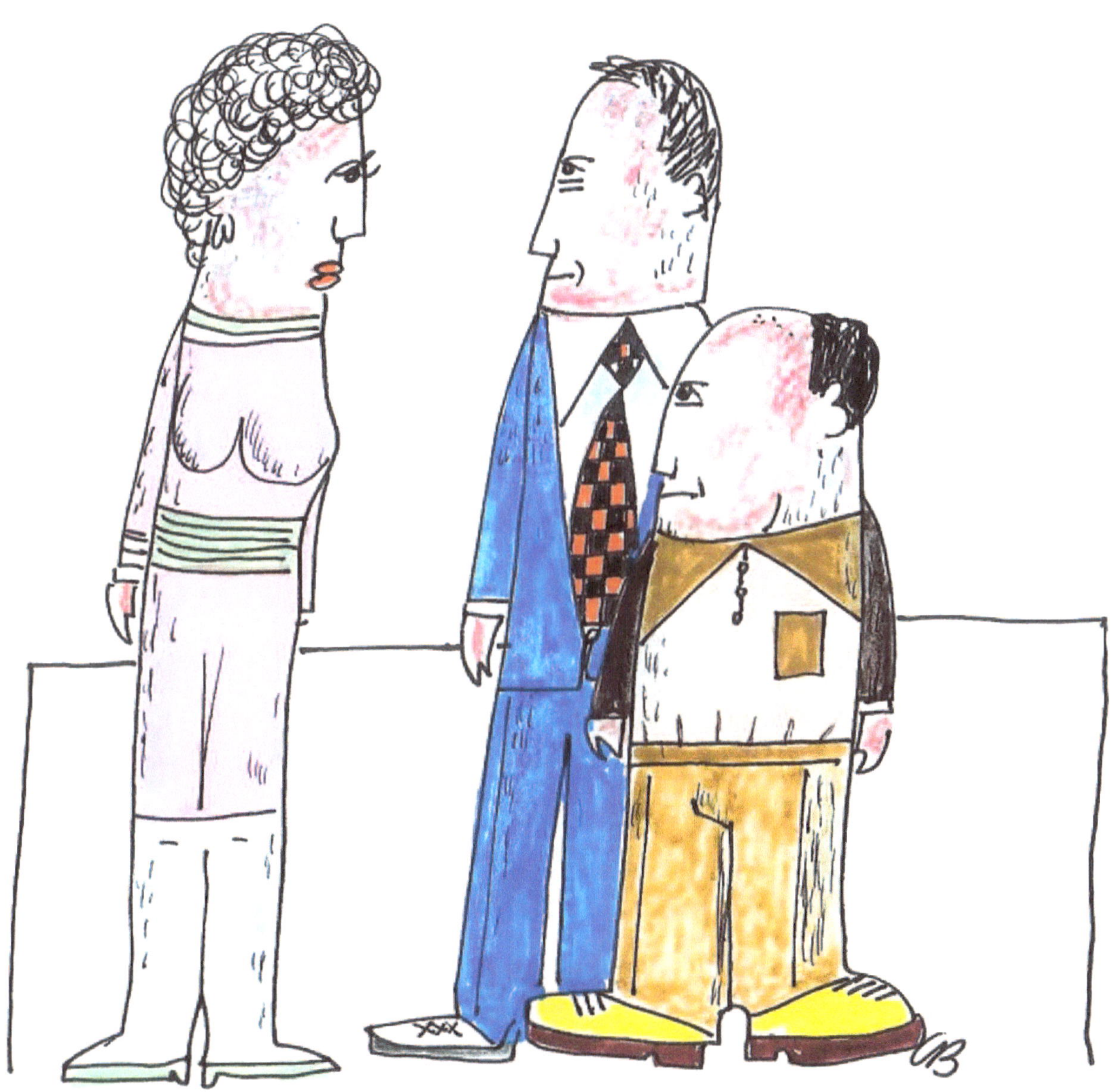

"This is Danny Devito. He's angry...and he bites!"

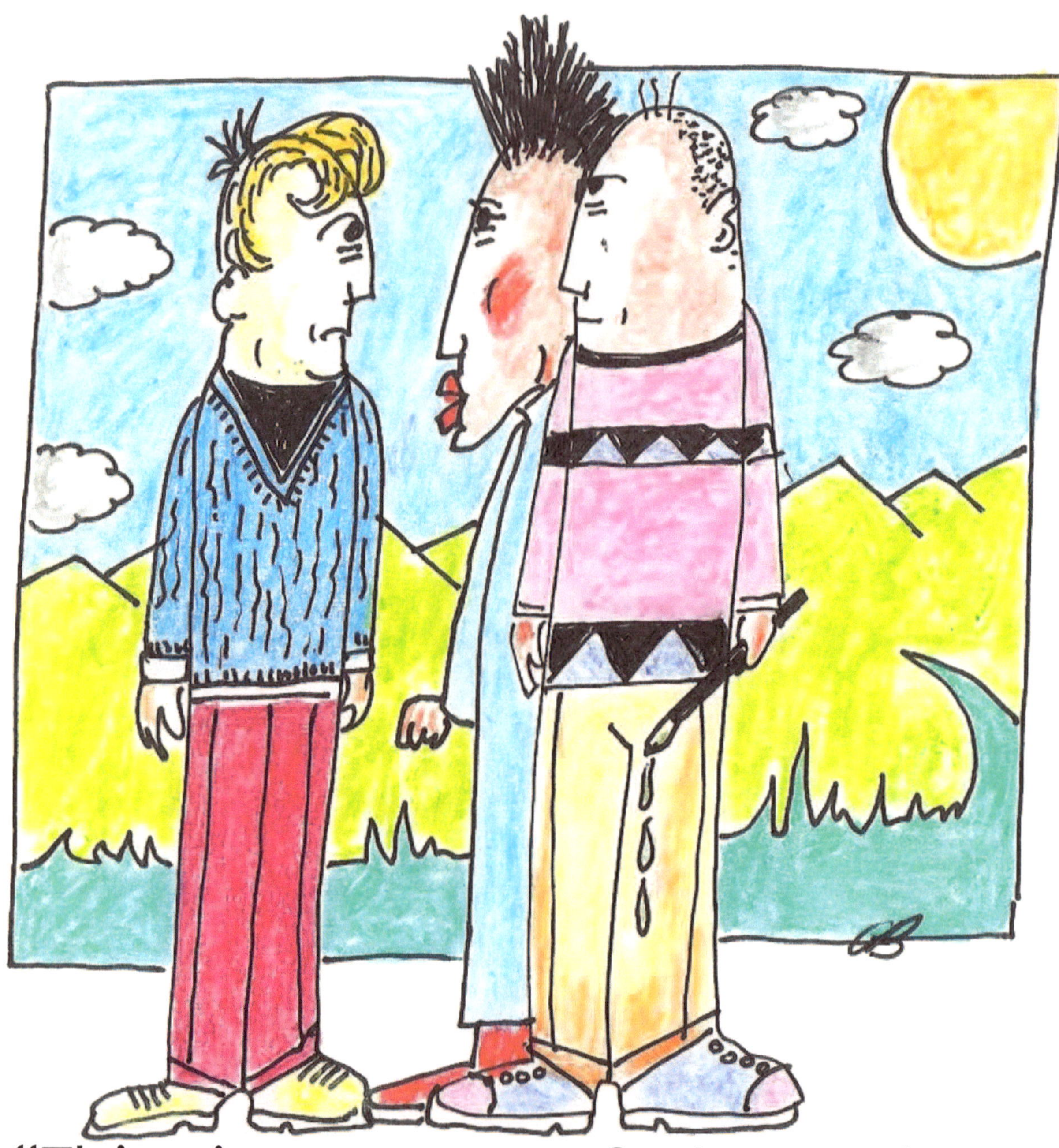

“This is your new father Peirre.
He paints & likes my money.”

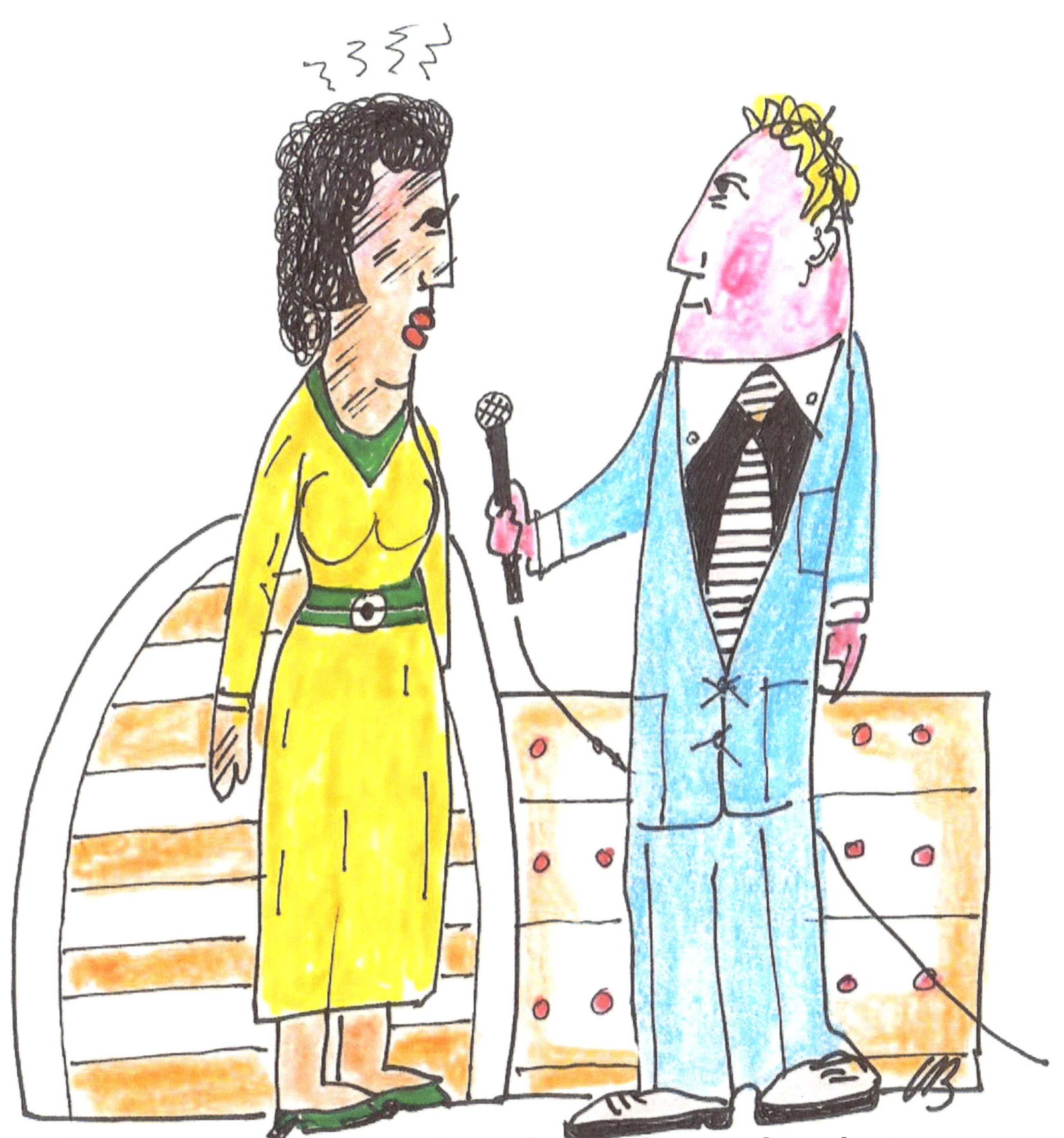

"I went so viral, they had to call in a specialist in contagious diseases."

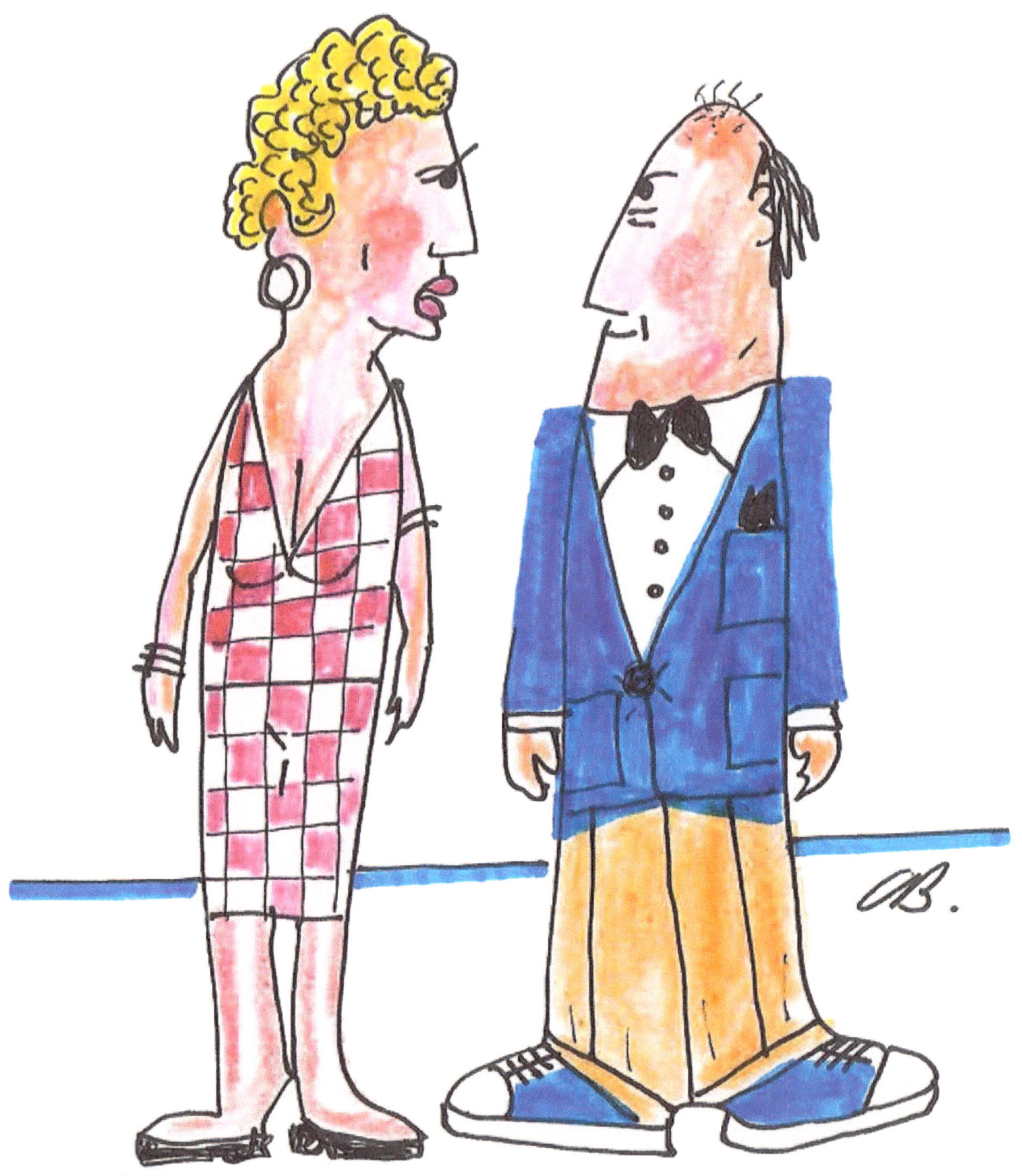

"I'll give up my Neiman Marcus card if you let me keep my Tennis Pro."

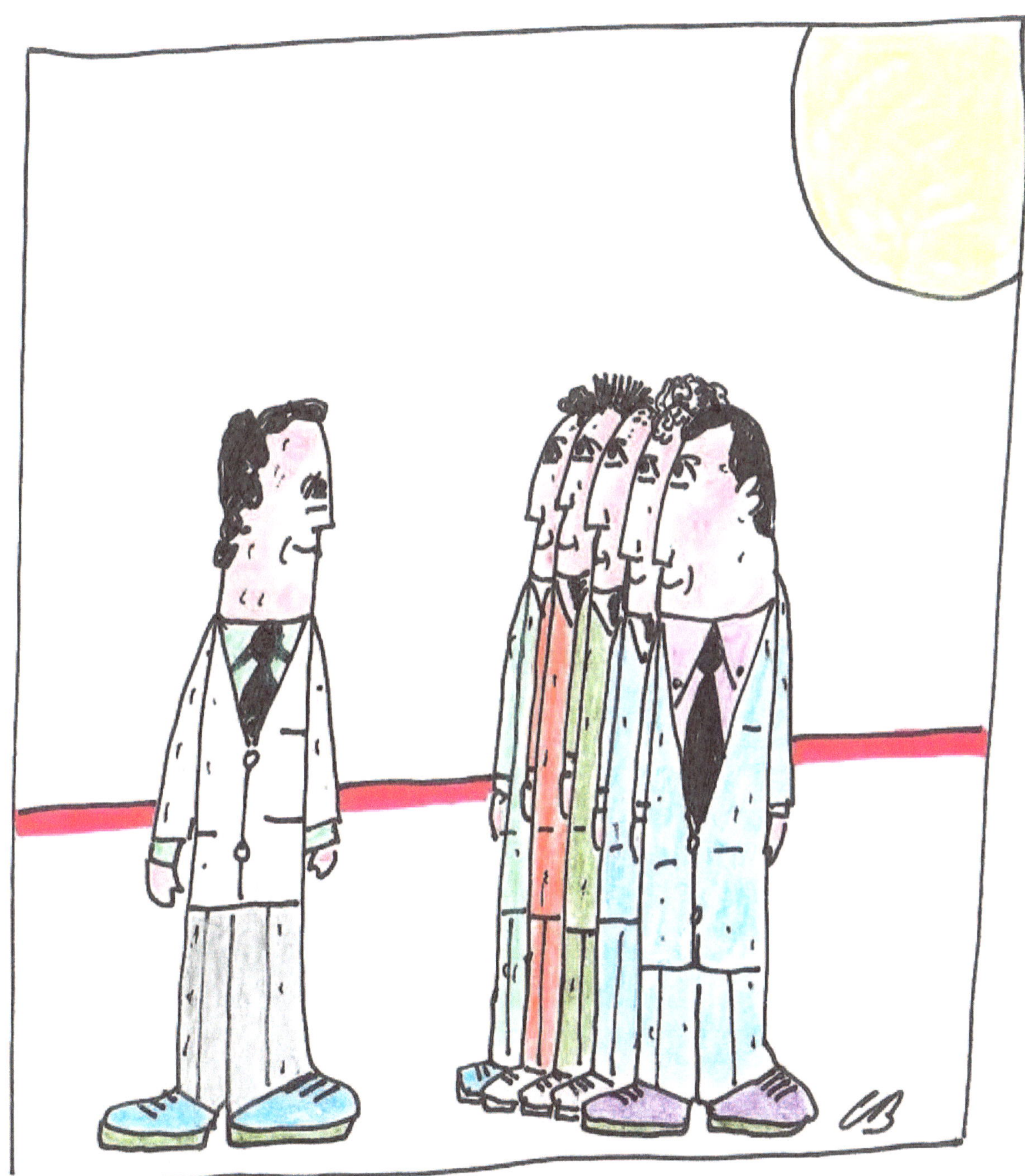

"Okay fellow Republicans...get out there & be unreasonable."

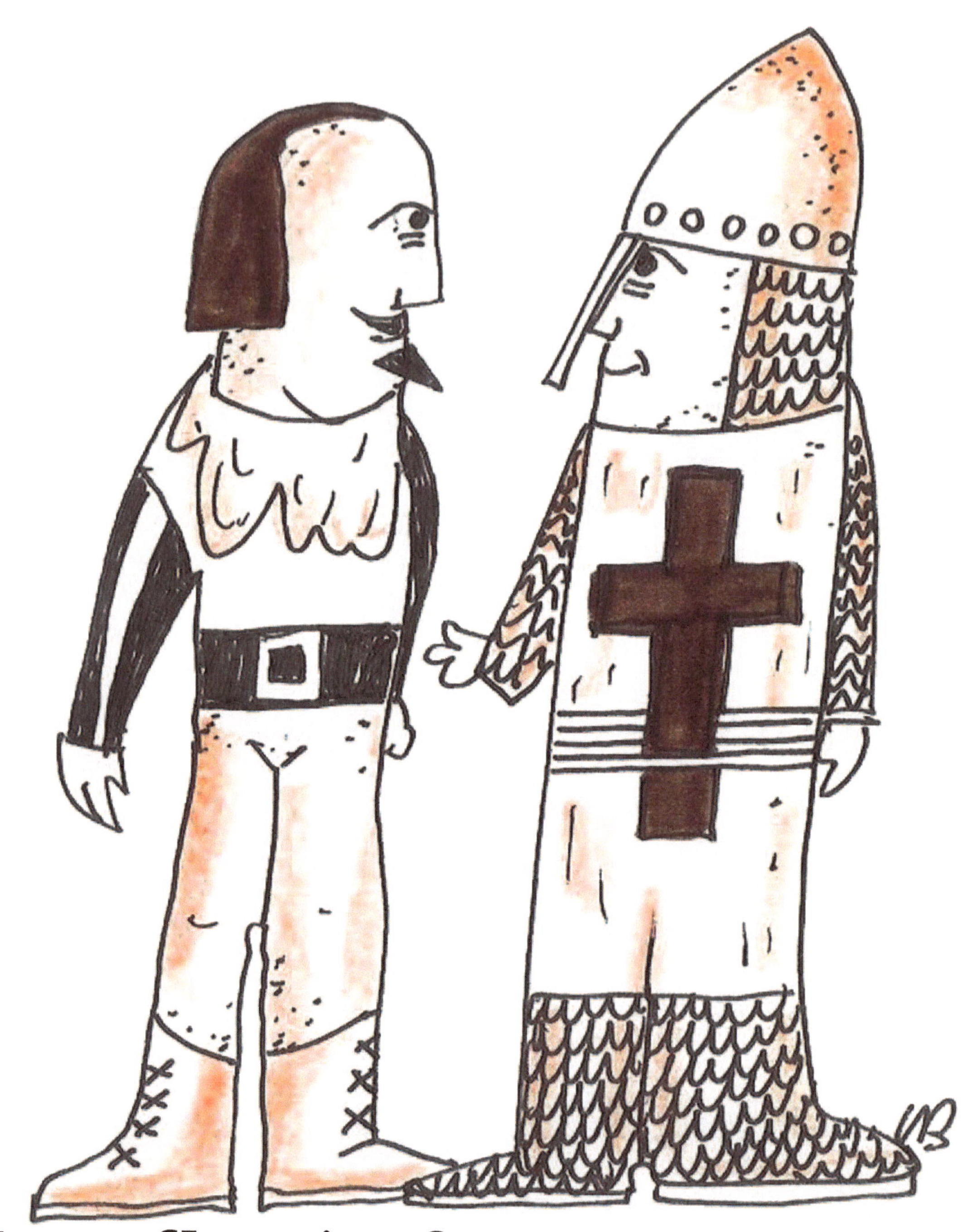

“Just flew in from the Crusades, and boy are my arms tired!!”

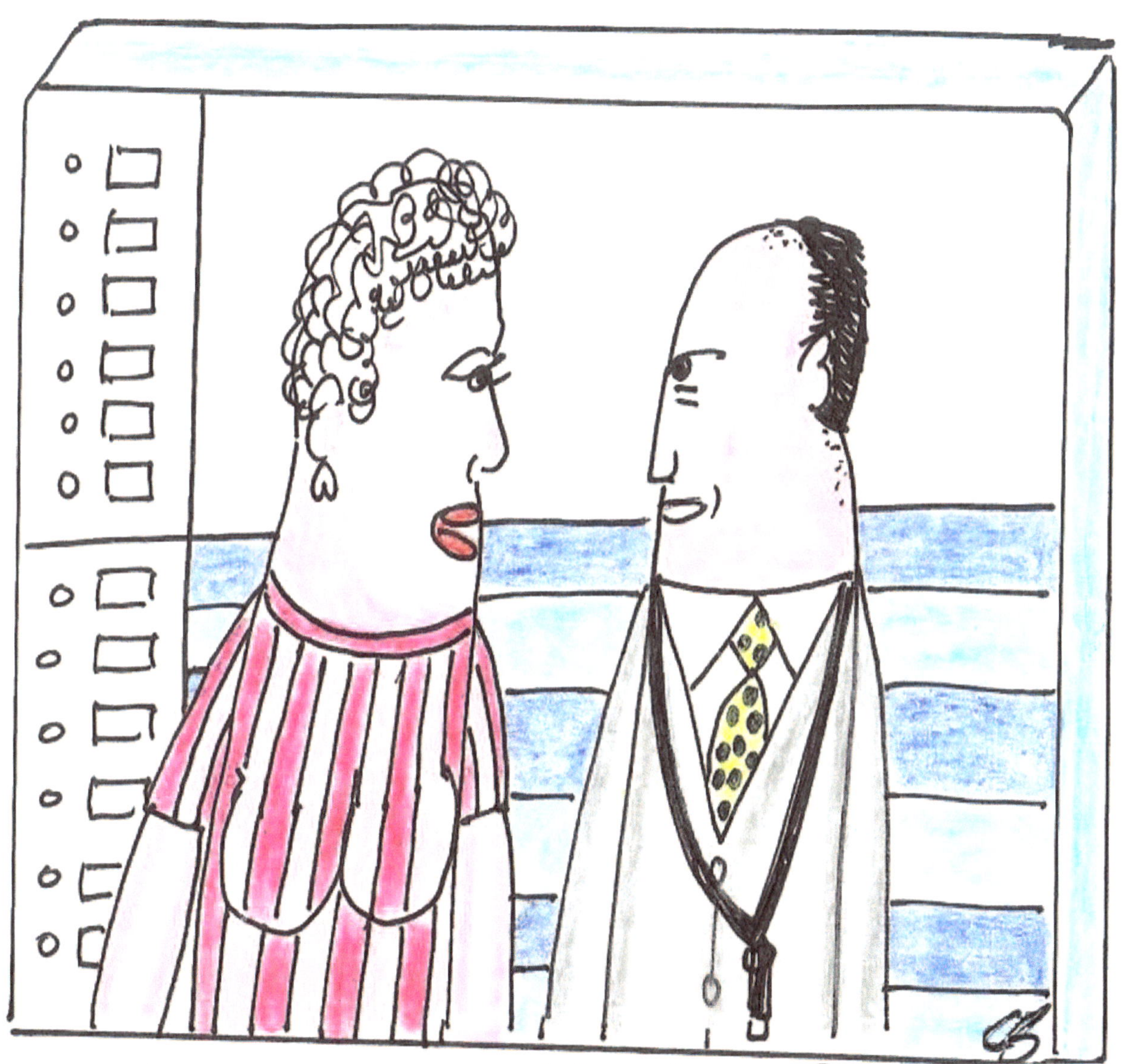

"You are suffering from a sprained relationship."

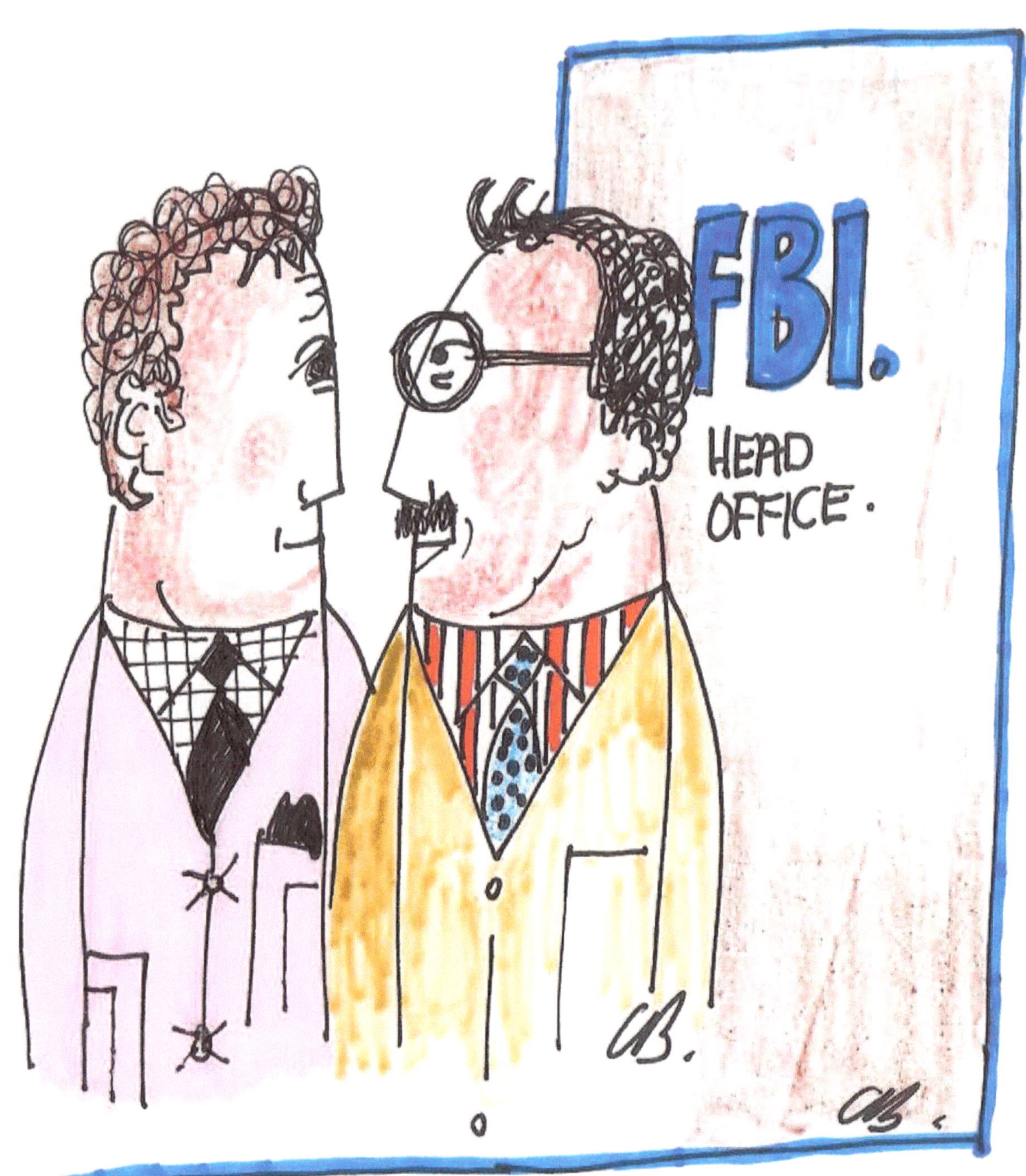

"Your job, Agent Farrell, is to find out if the CIA is as screwed up as we are!"

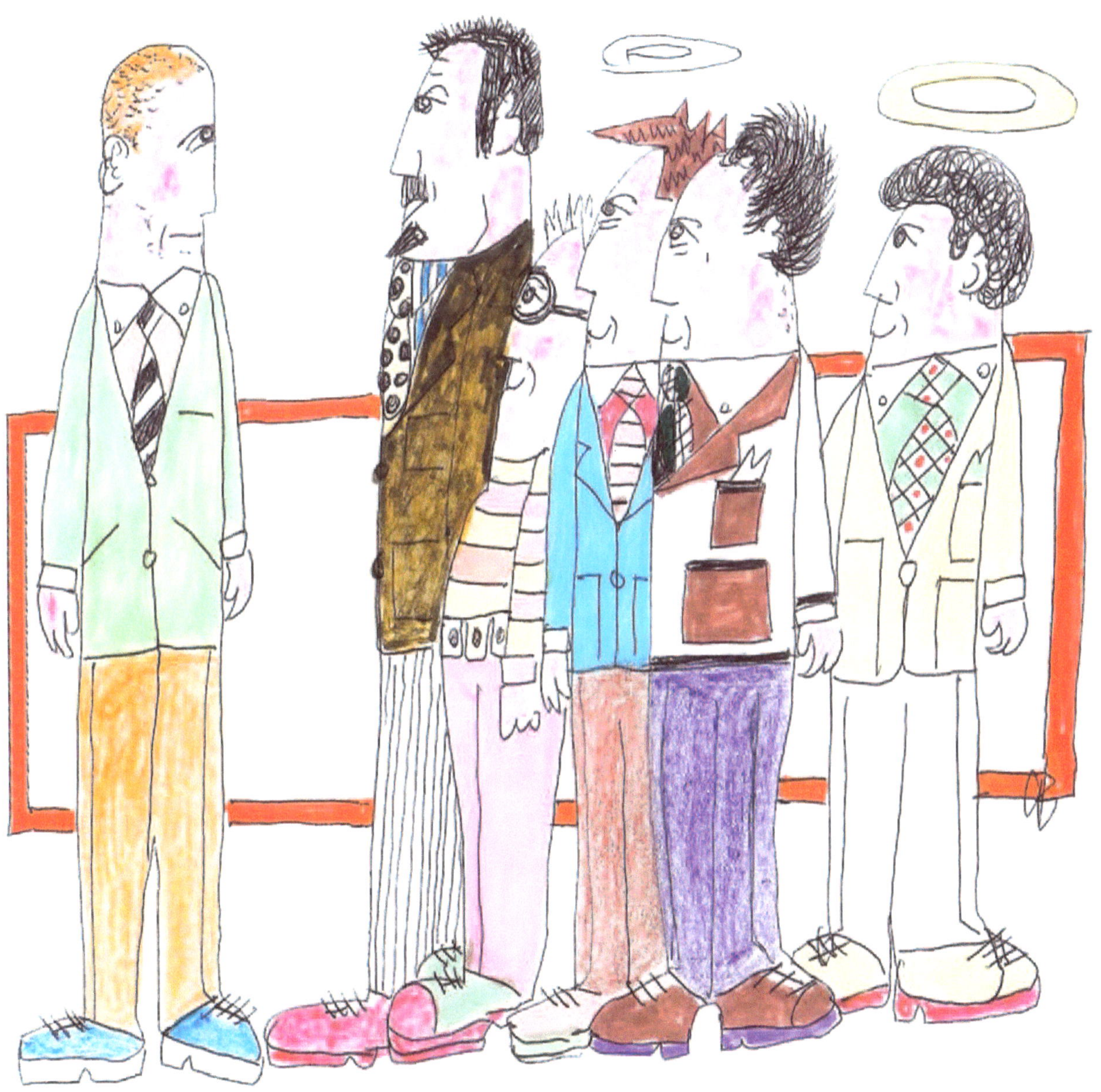

"So, who are the Evangelicals?"

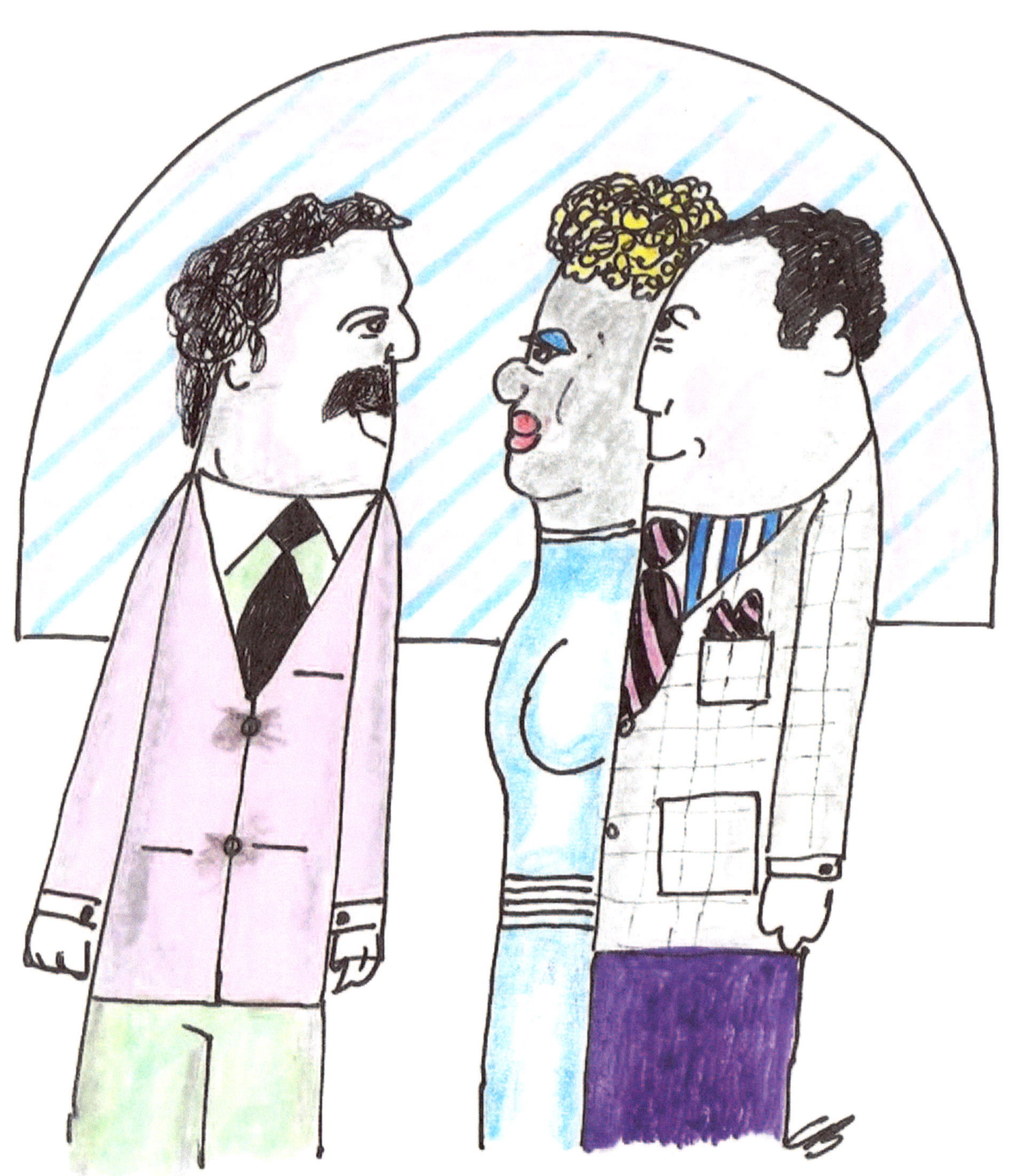

"Do you know anymore black people who aren't too black?"

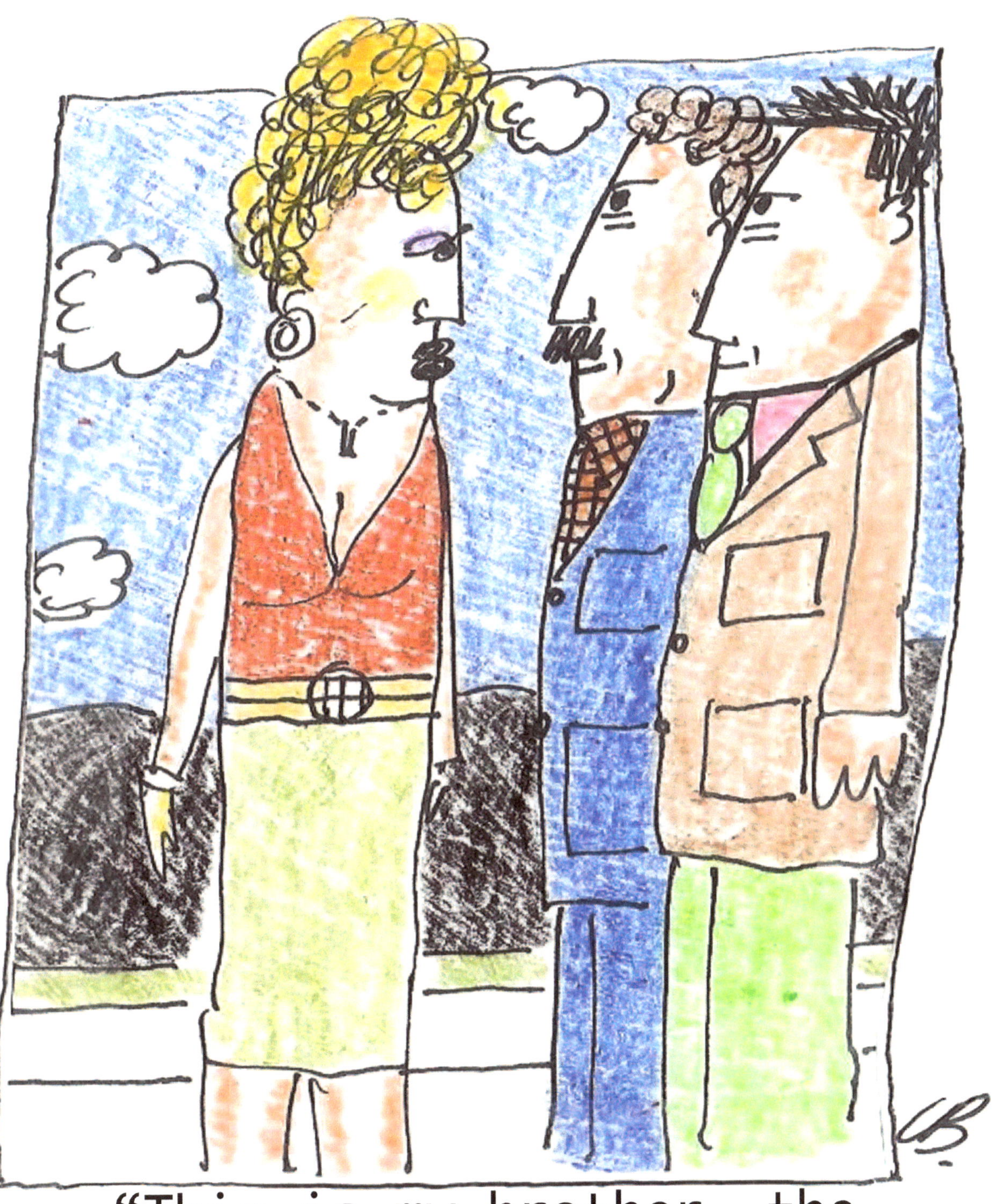

“This is my brother, the reformed corporate liar.”

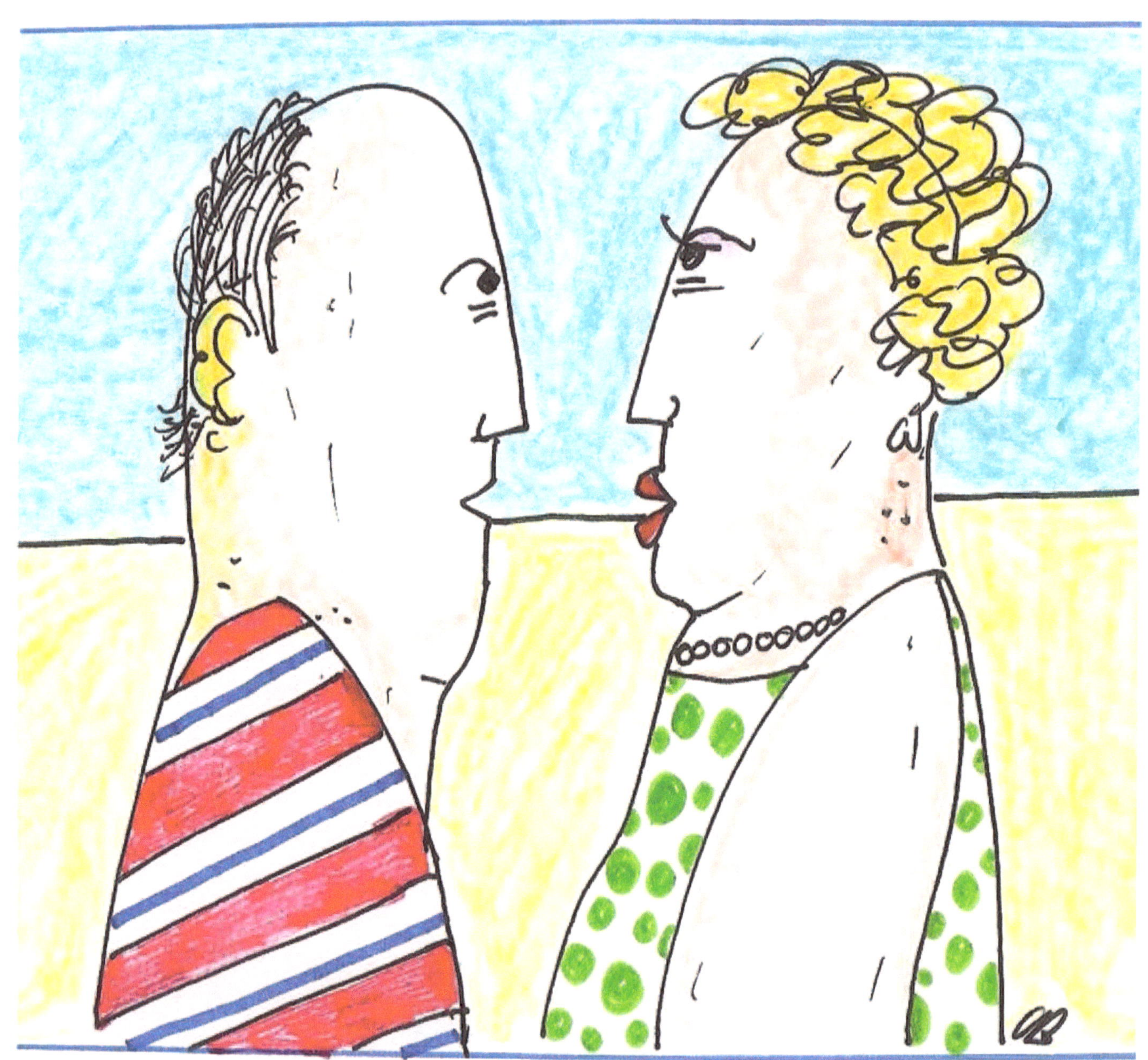

“I’m leaving you for a more meaningful Bank Card.”

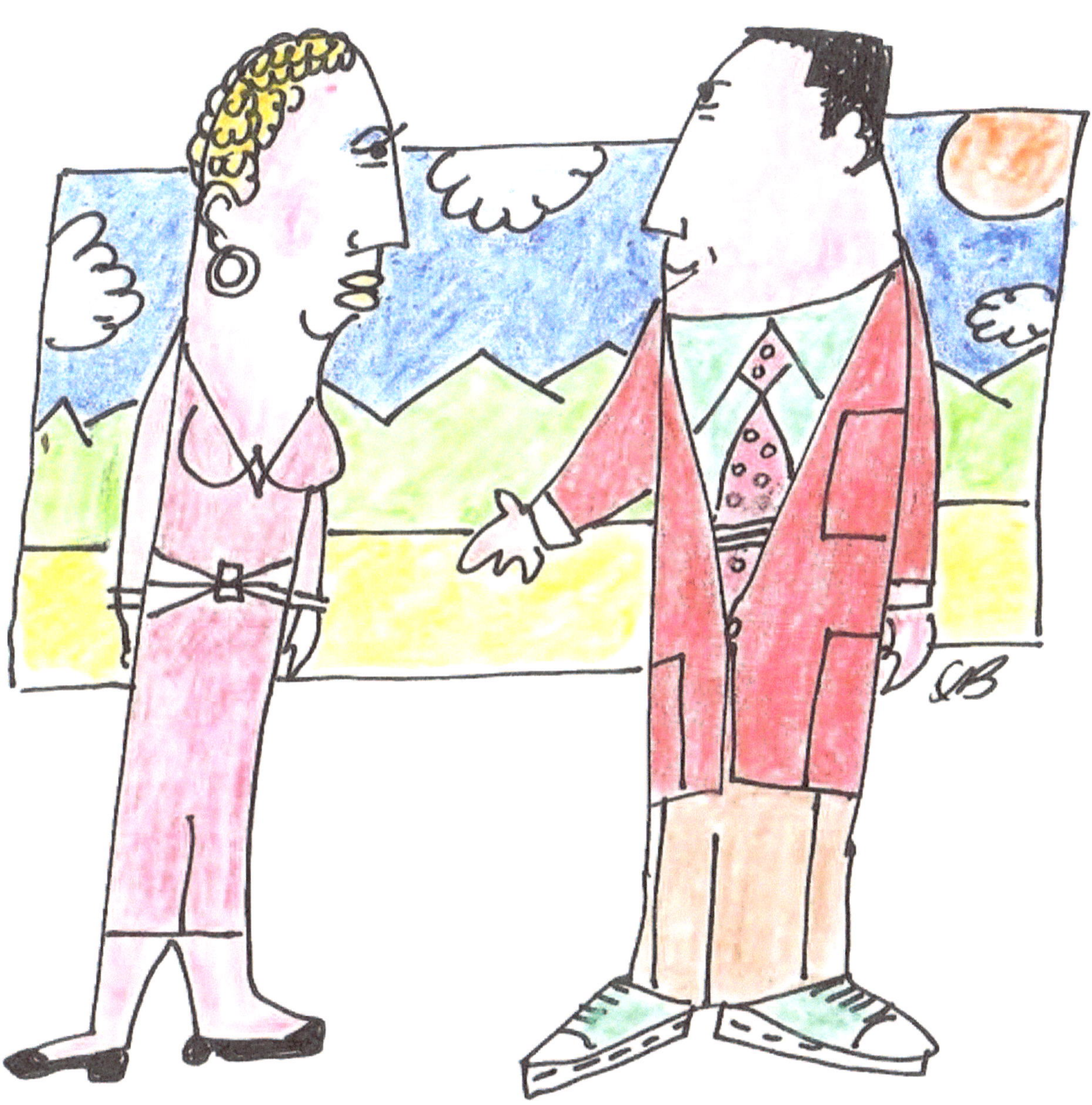

"We're both healthy adult people, so you'll go get a job & I'll help you look for it."

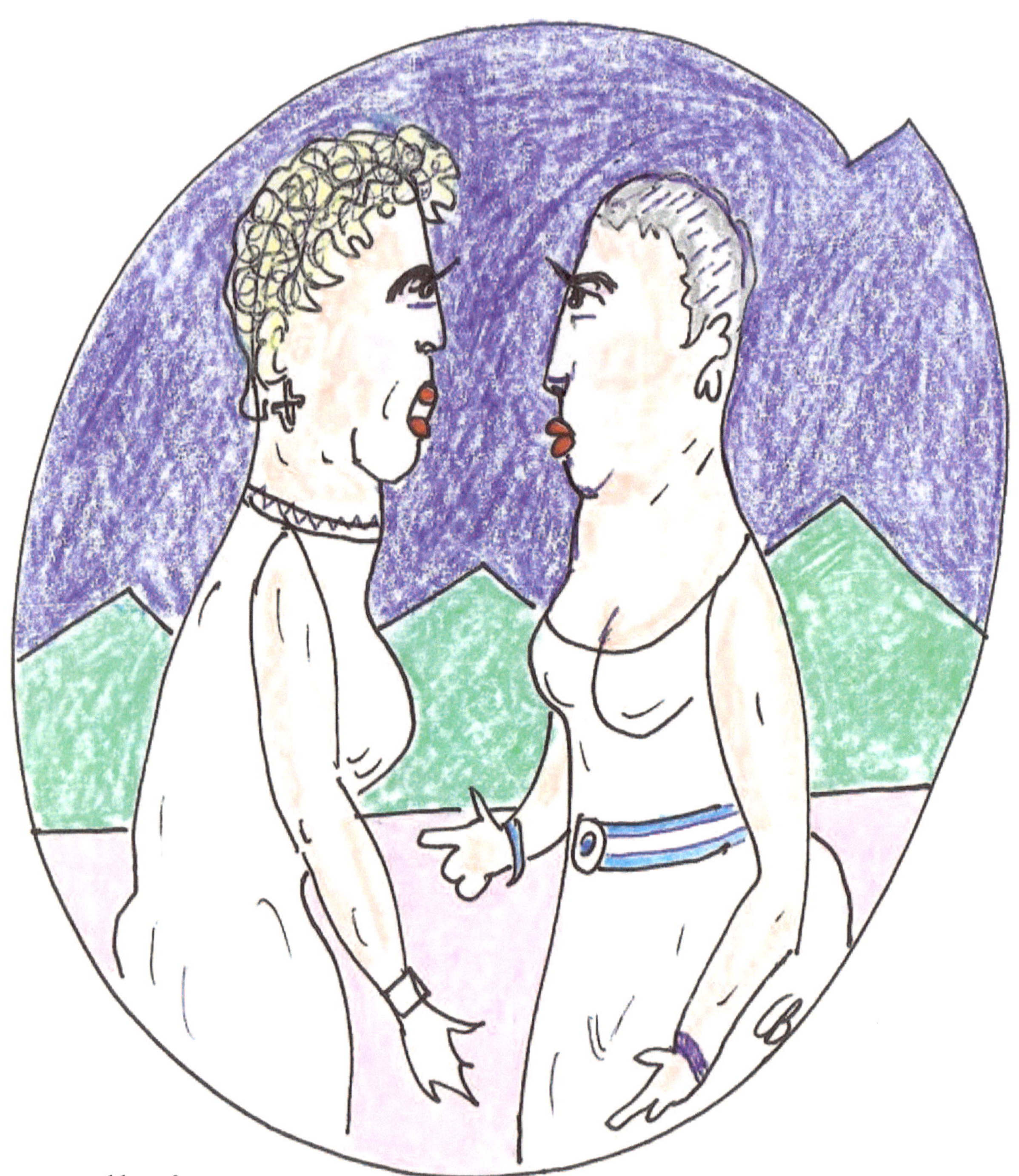

"I'm sending my husband to obedience school."

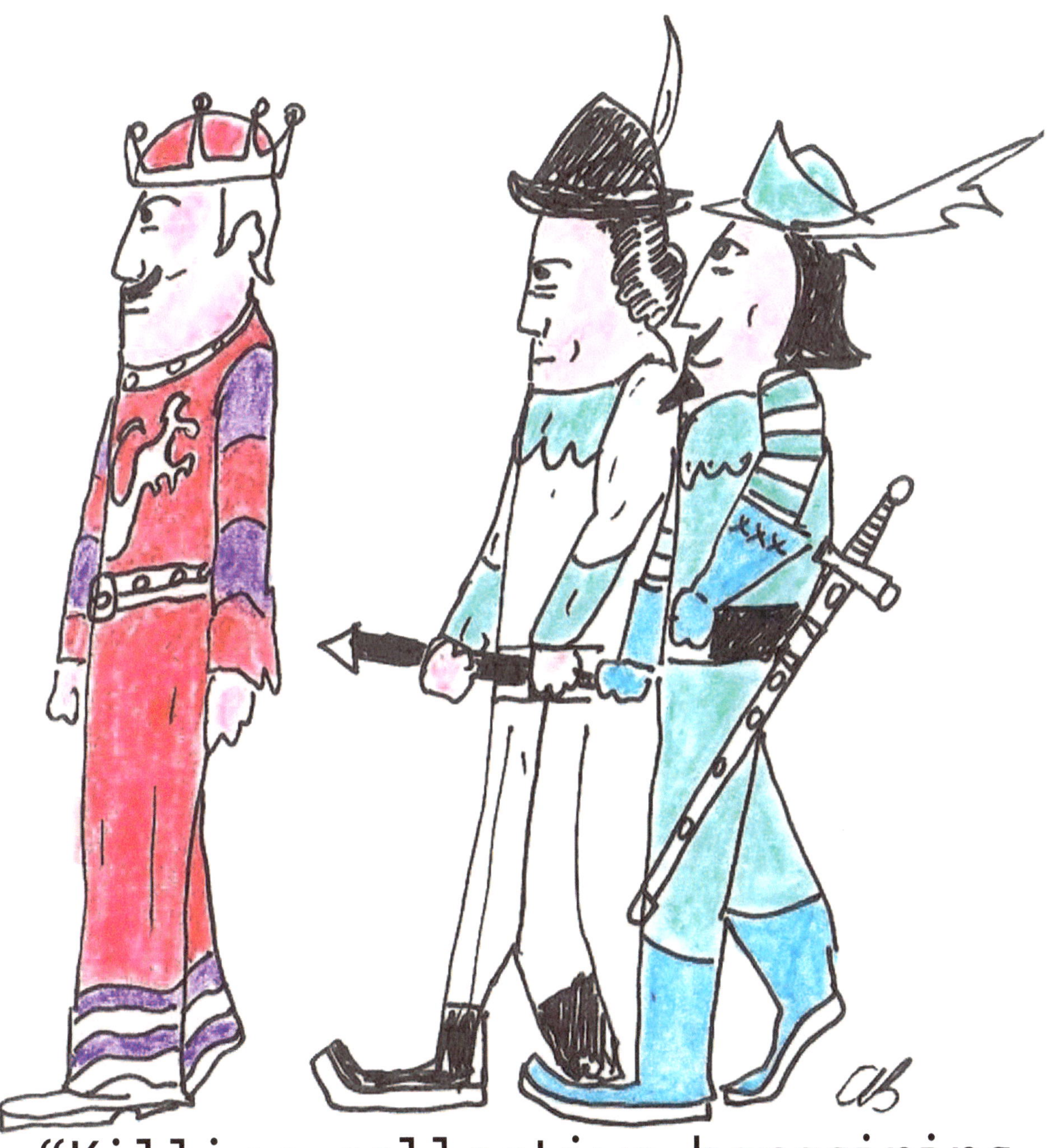

"Killing collective bargaining for the Merry Men was the final straw King John."

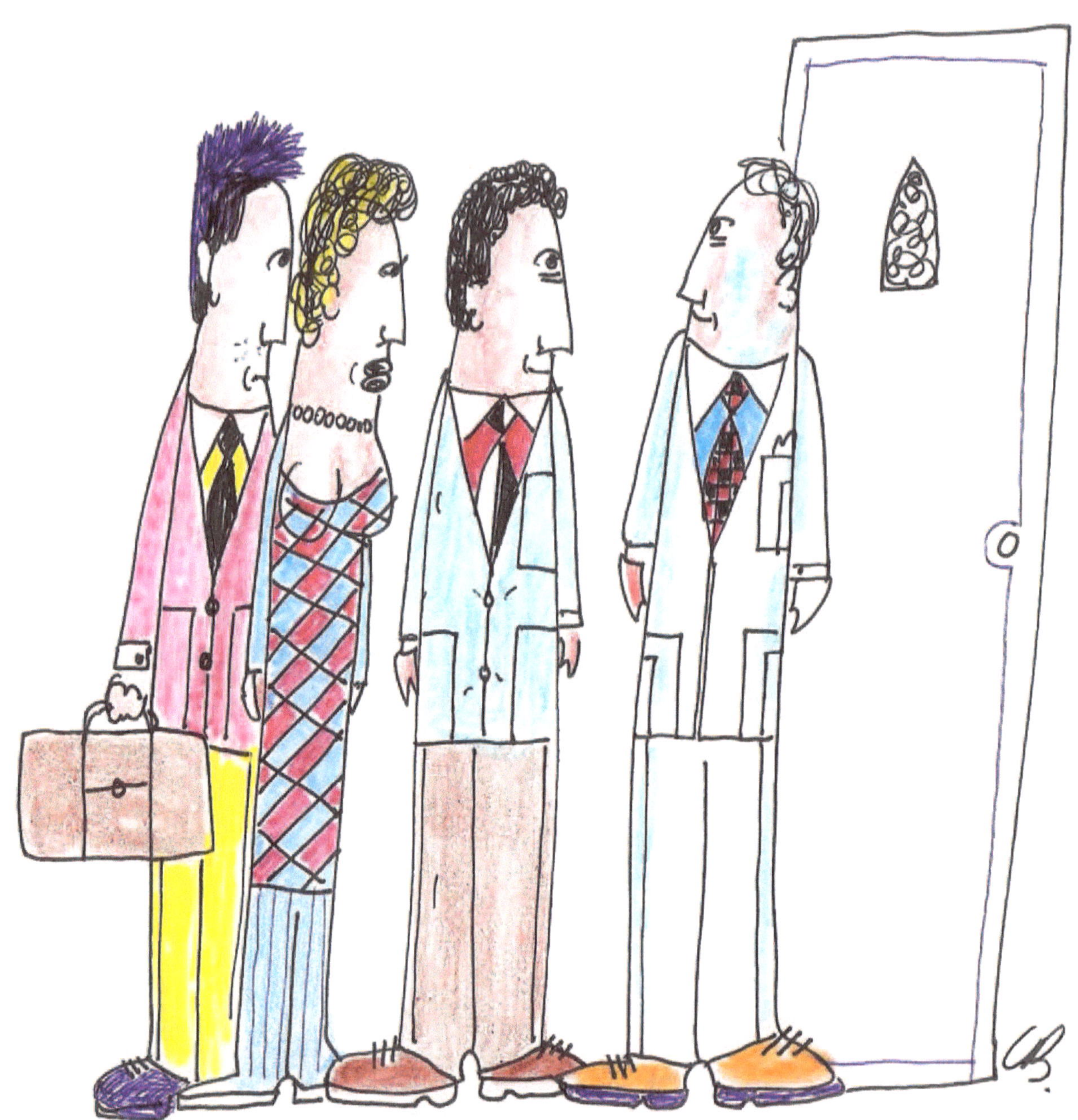

"This is Mr. & Mrs. Berkley. They lost their house & their savings. They want to spit on Wall Street."

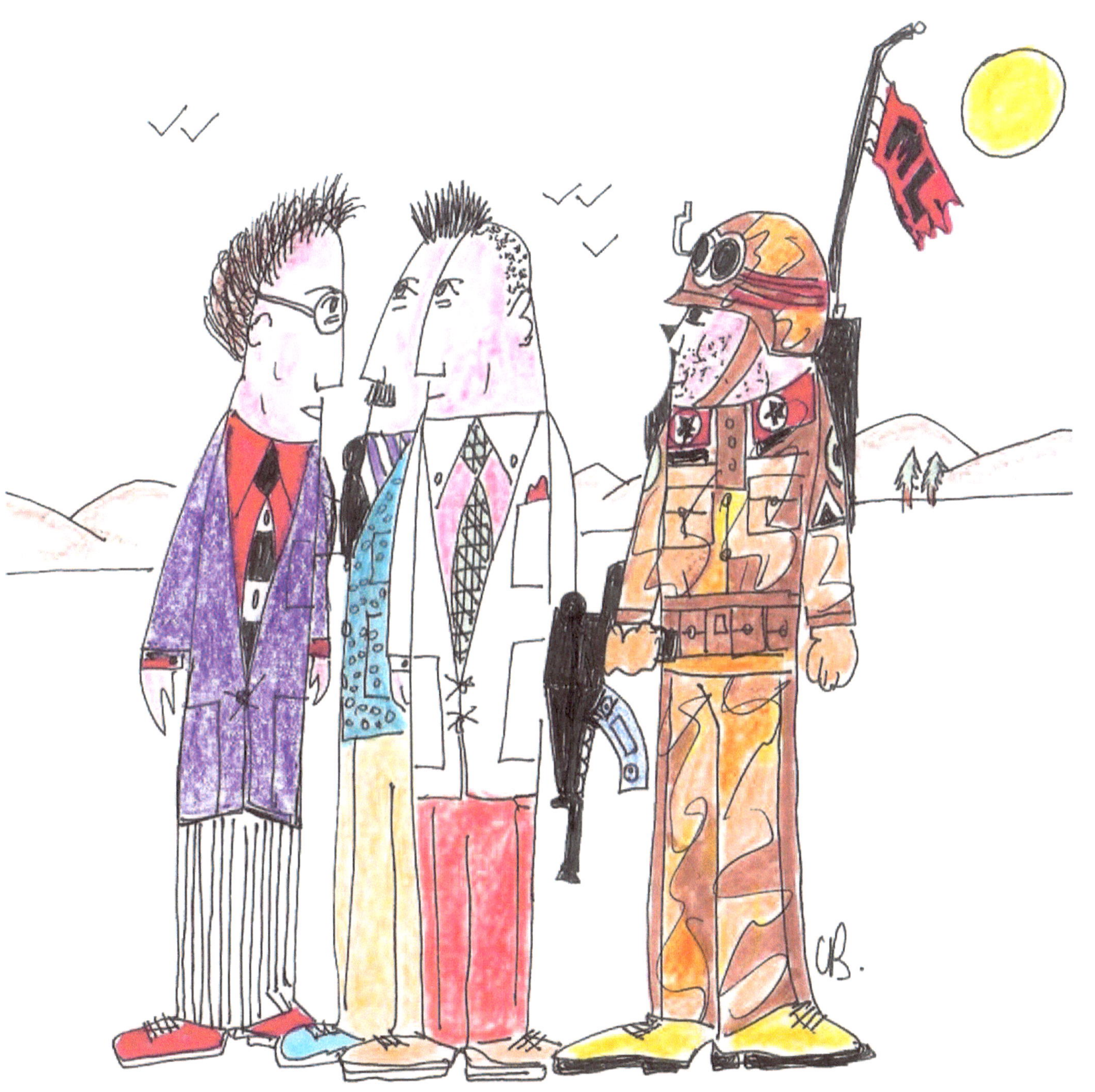

"This is a prototype of the Fox News Militia uniforms."

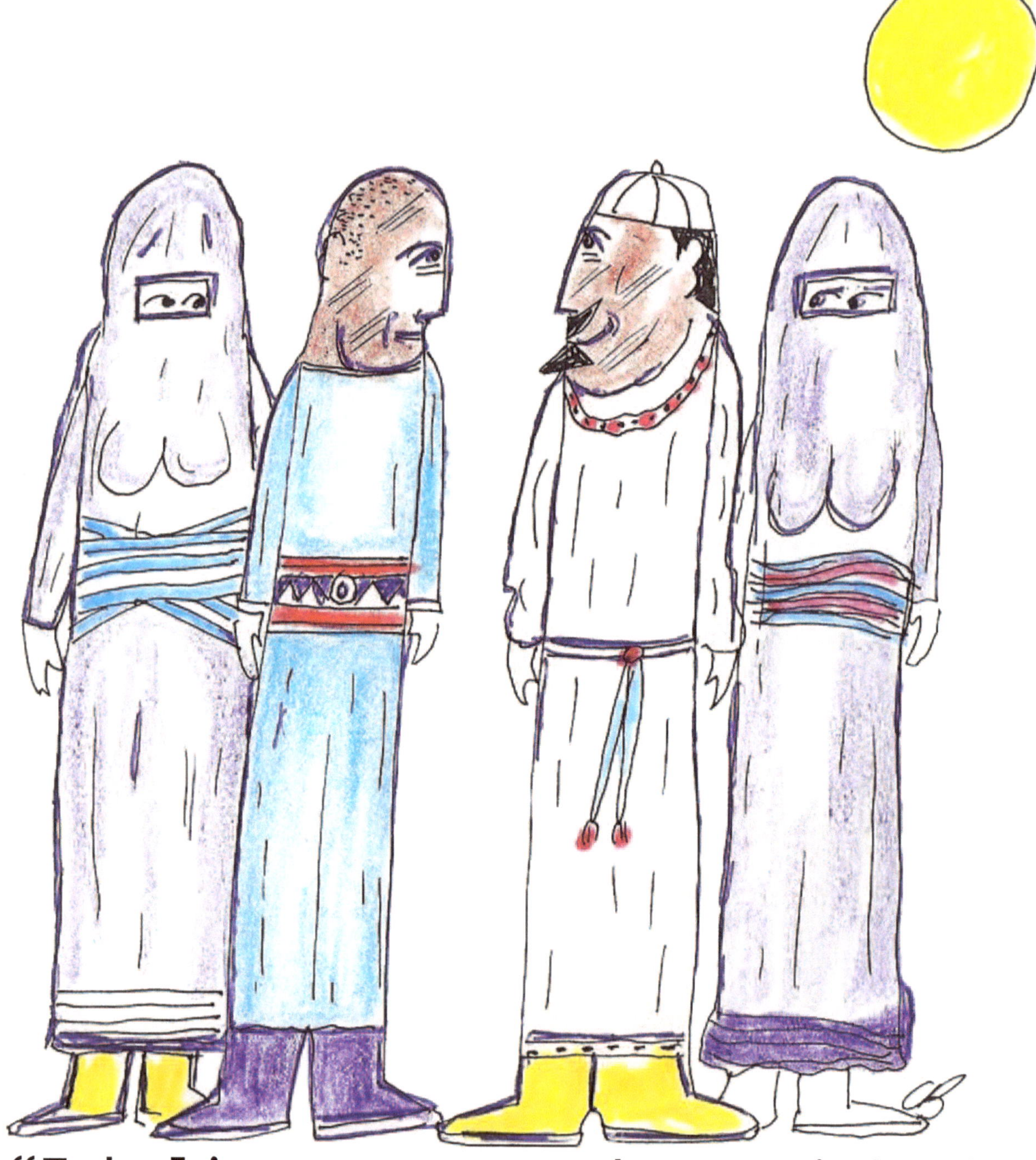

"I believe we went home with the wrong wives last night."

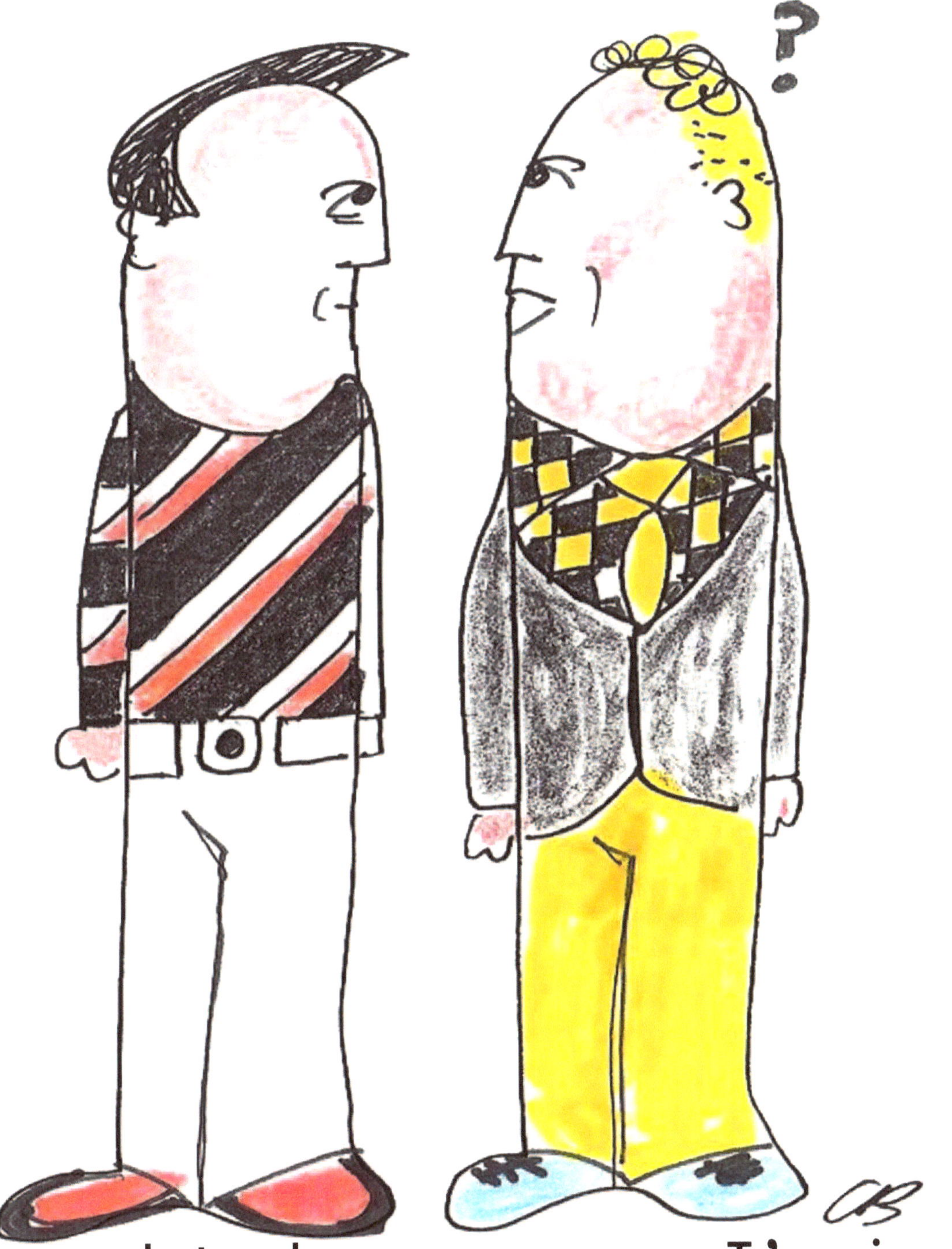

“I used to be gay...now I’m just funny!”

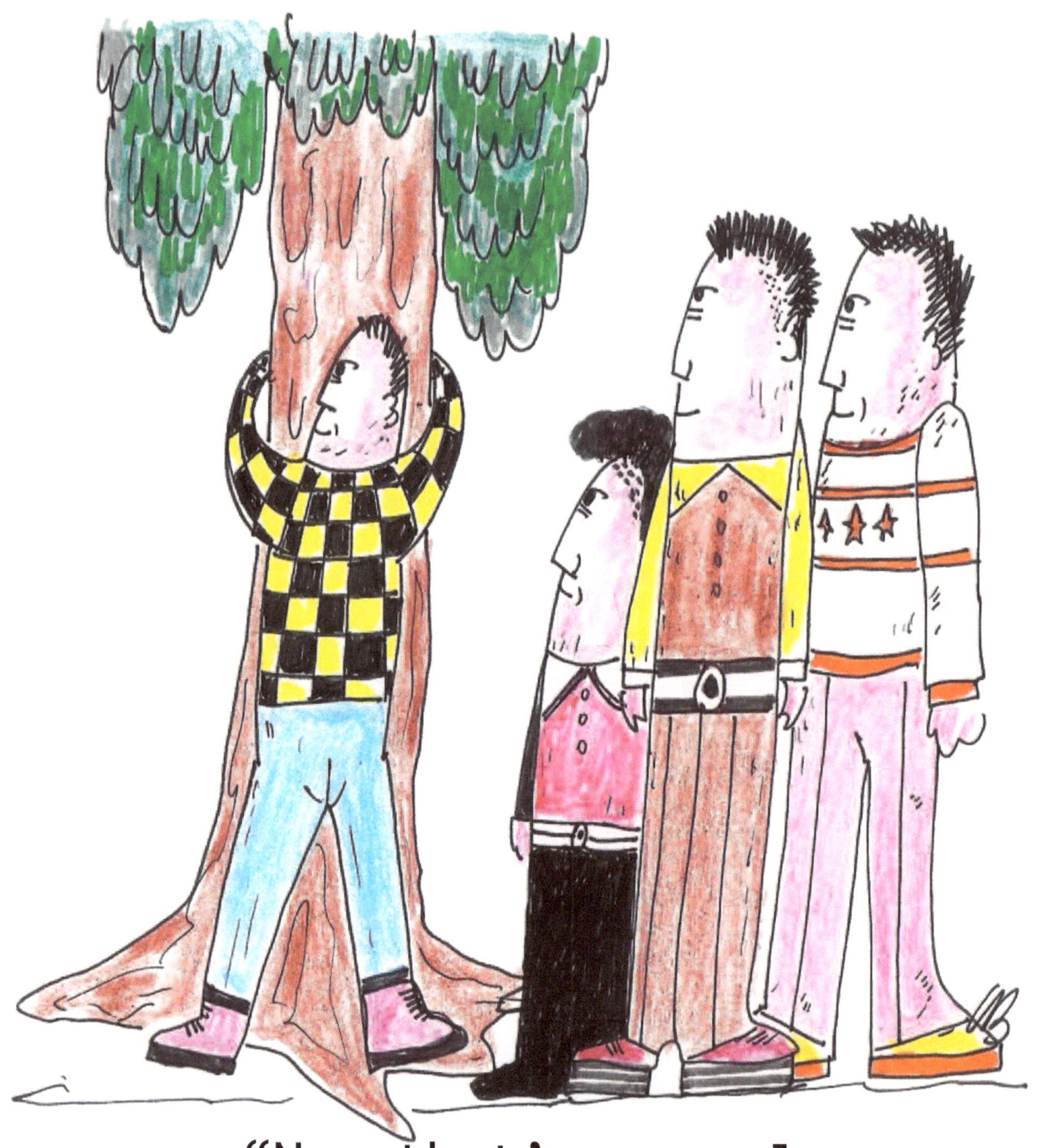

"Now that's a real Environmentalist!"

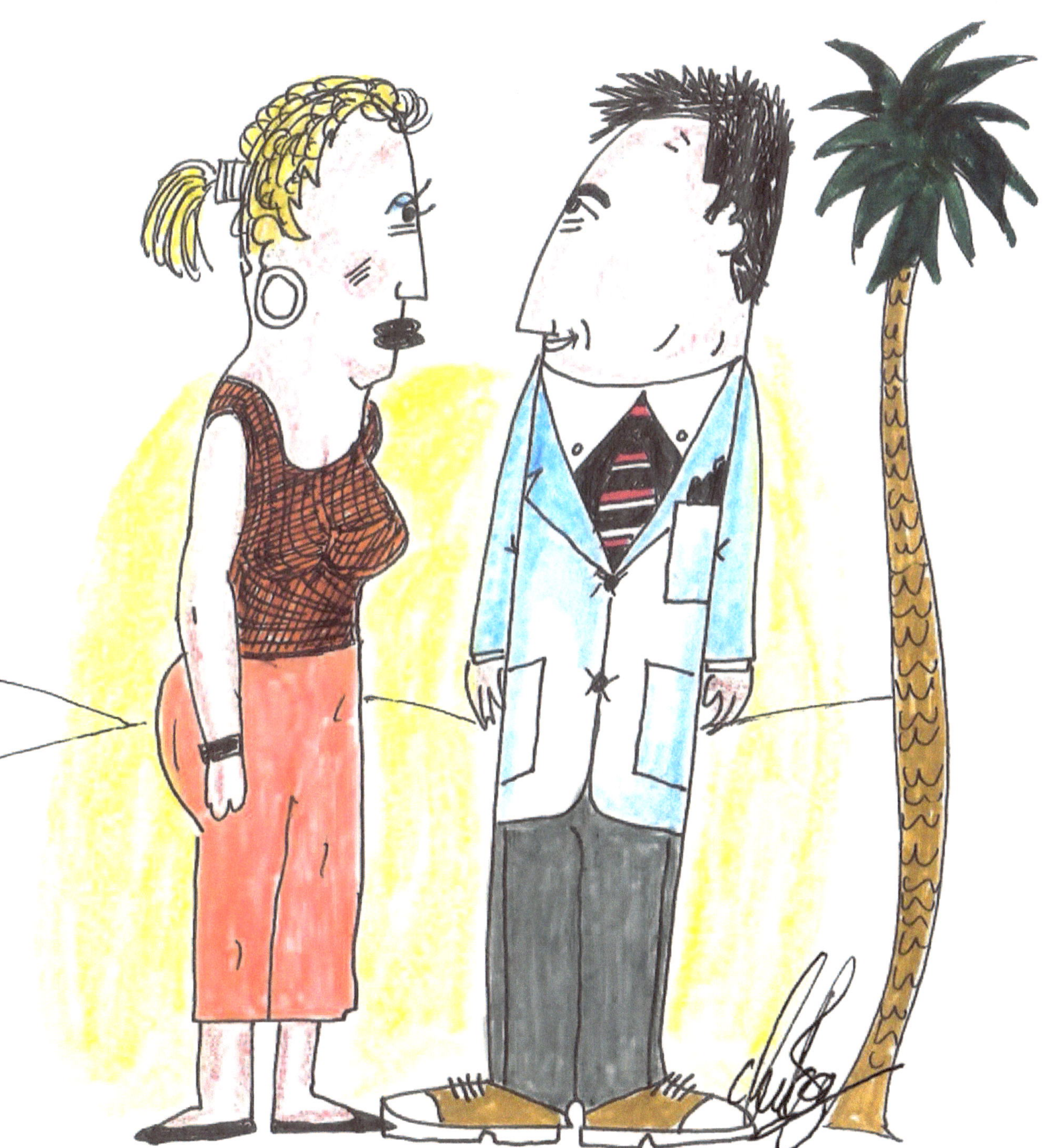

"I've fallen in love with myself again..."

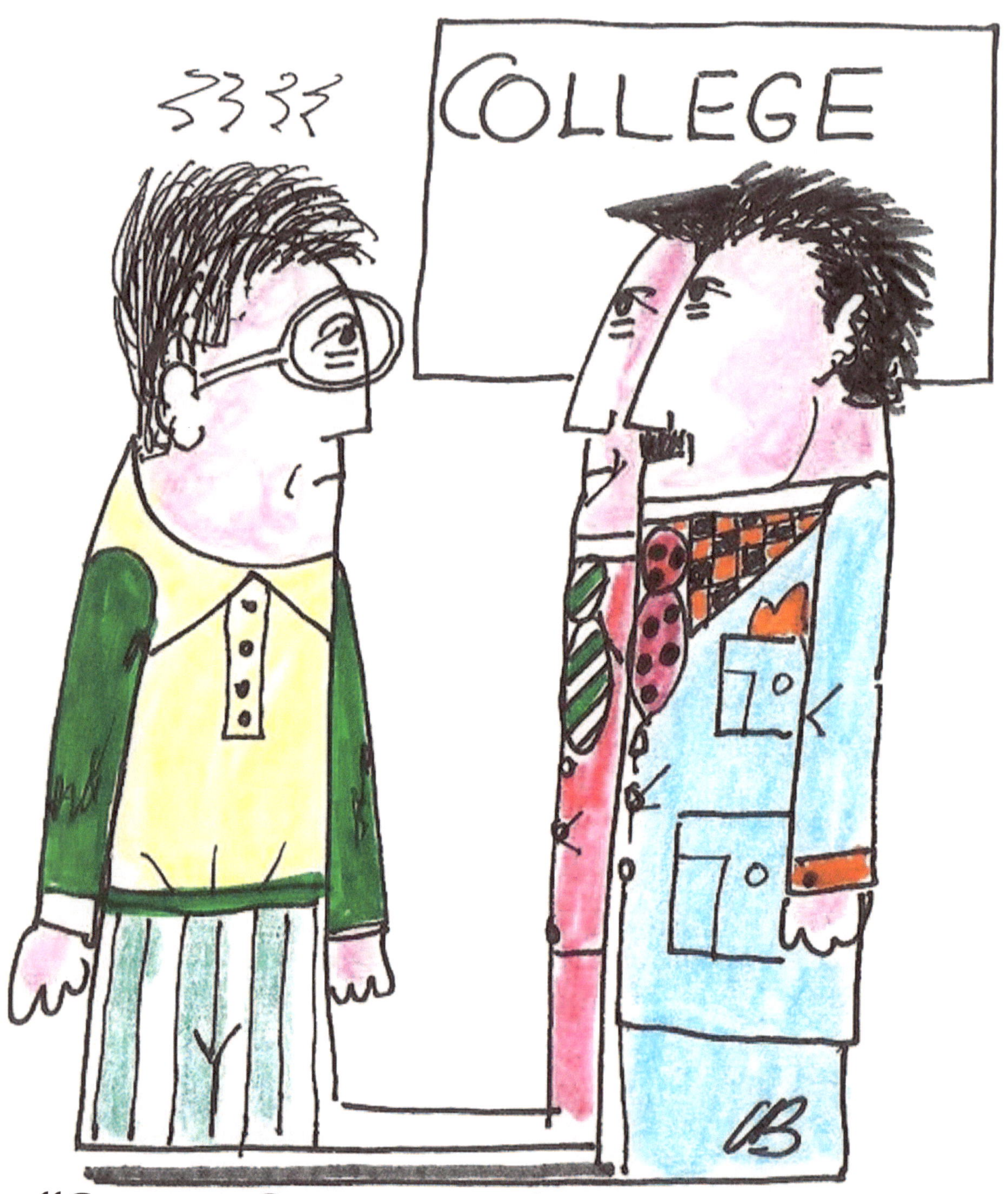

"Sorry Seymour, but some other kid already invented Facebook!"

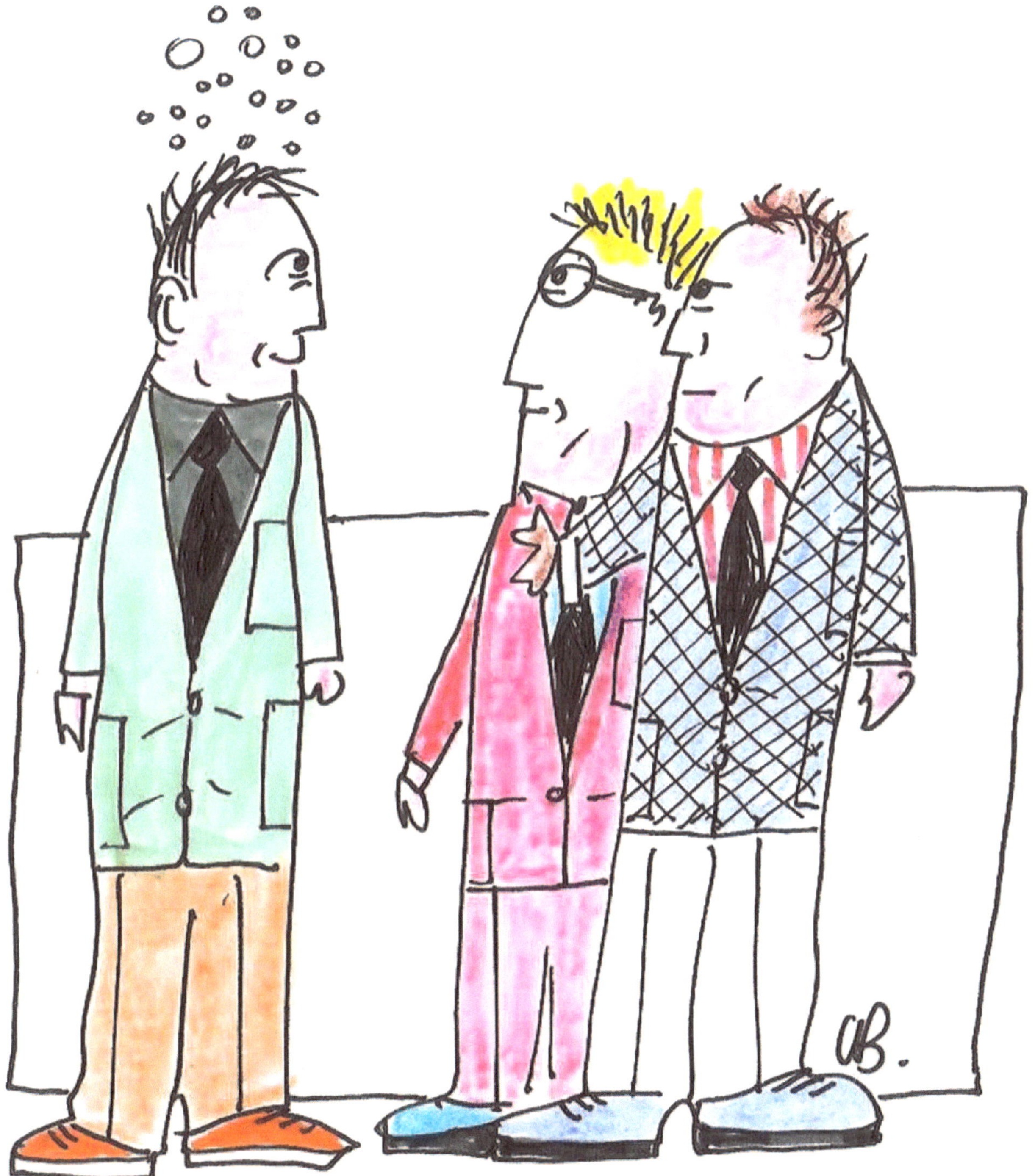

“This is my brother Bert...He’s a fugitive accountant.”

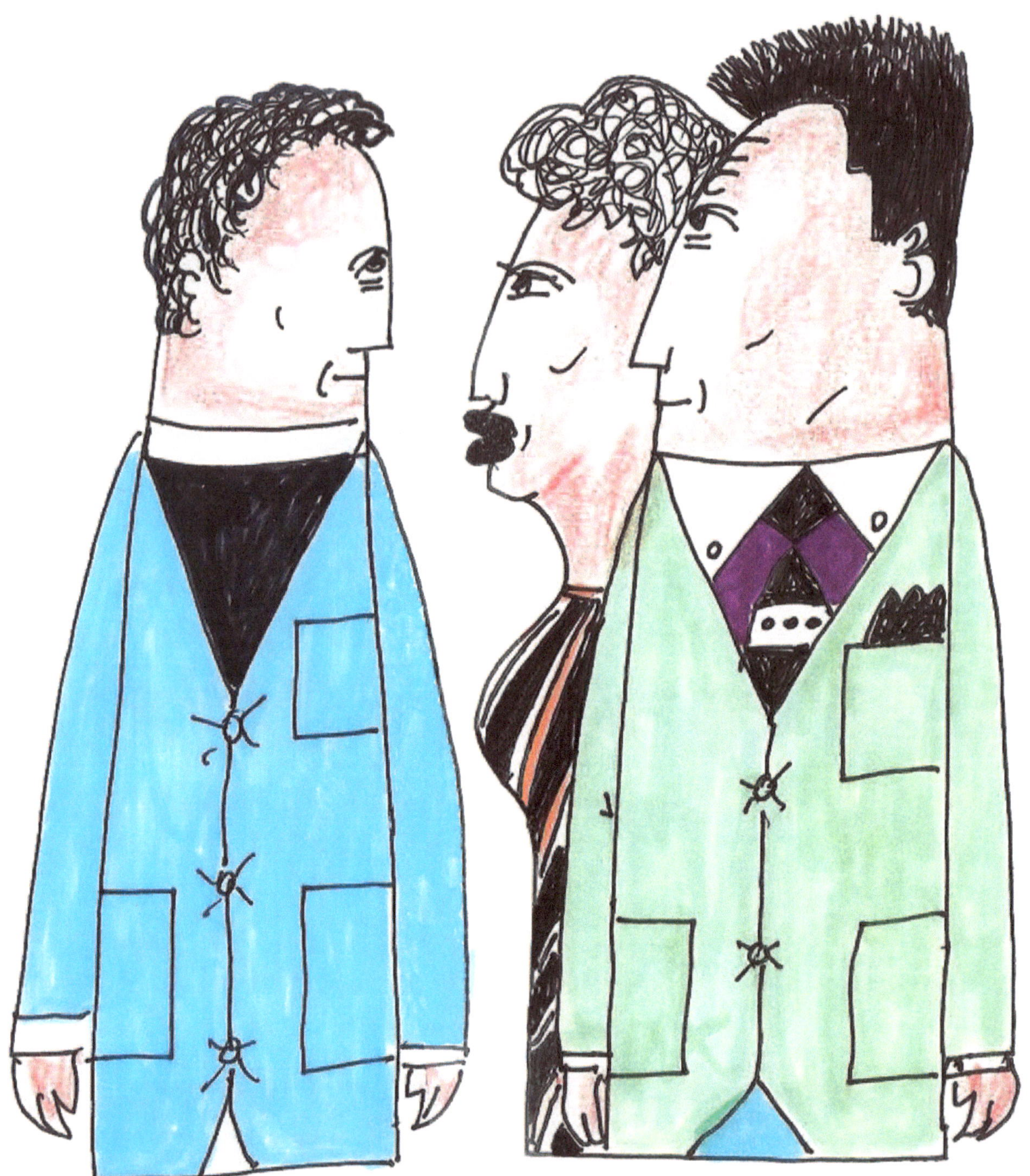

"I think I might have got a text from God last night. Or it might have been my sister."

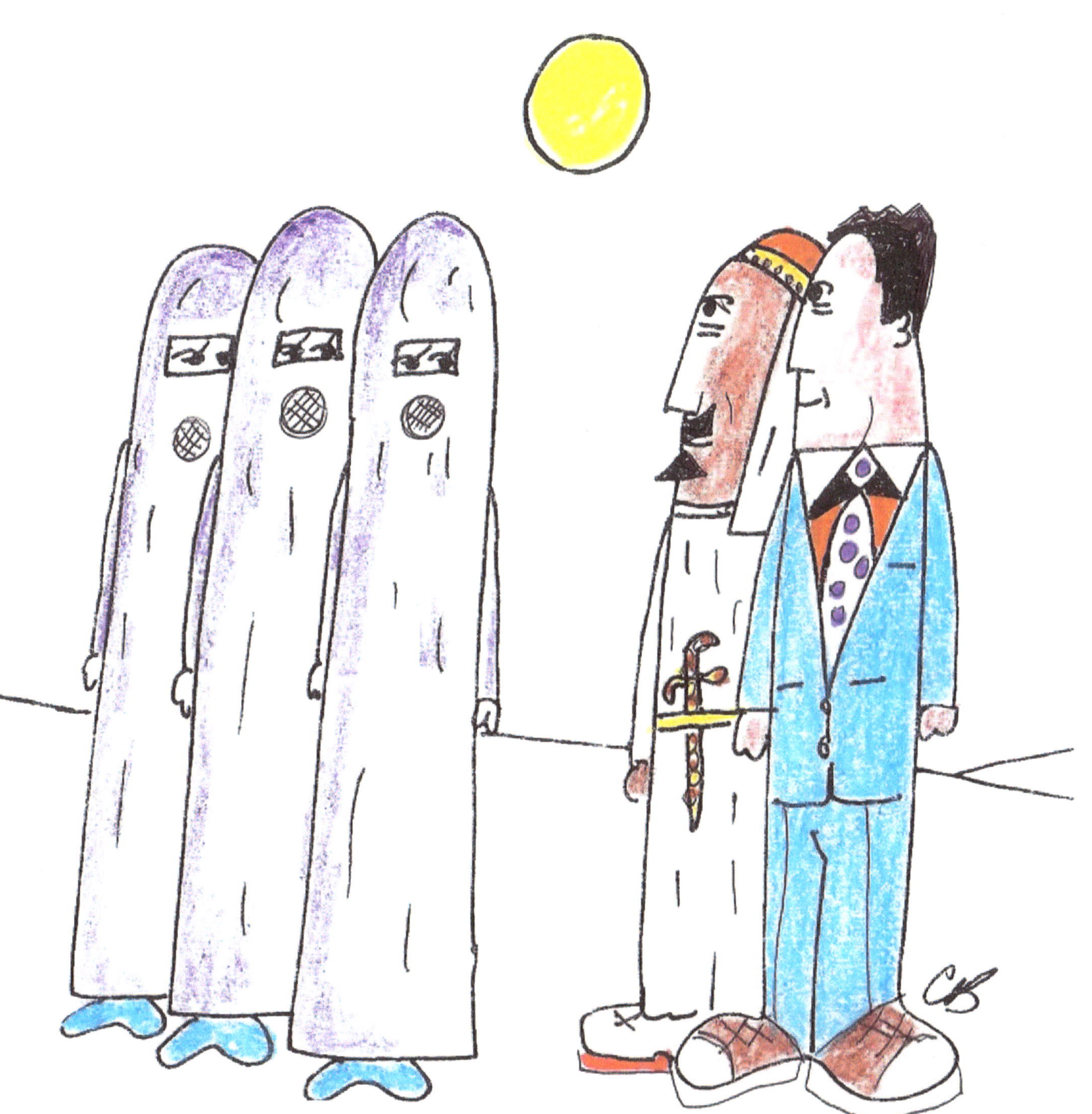

“Your majesty...may I present The Dixie Chicks.”

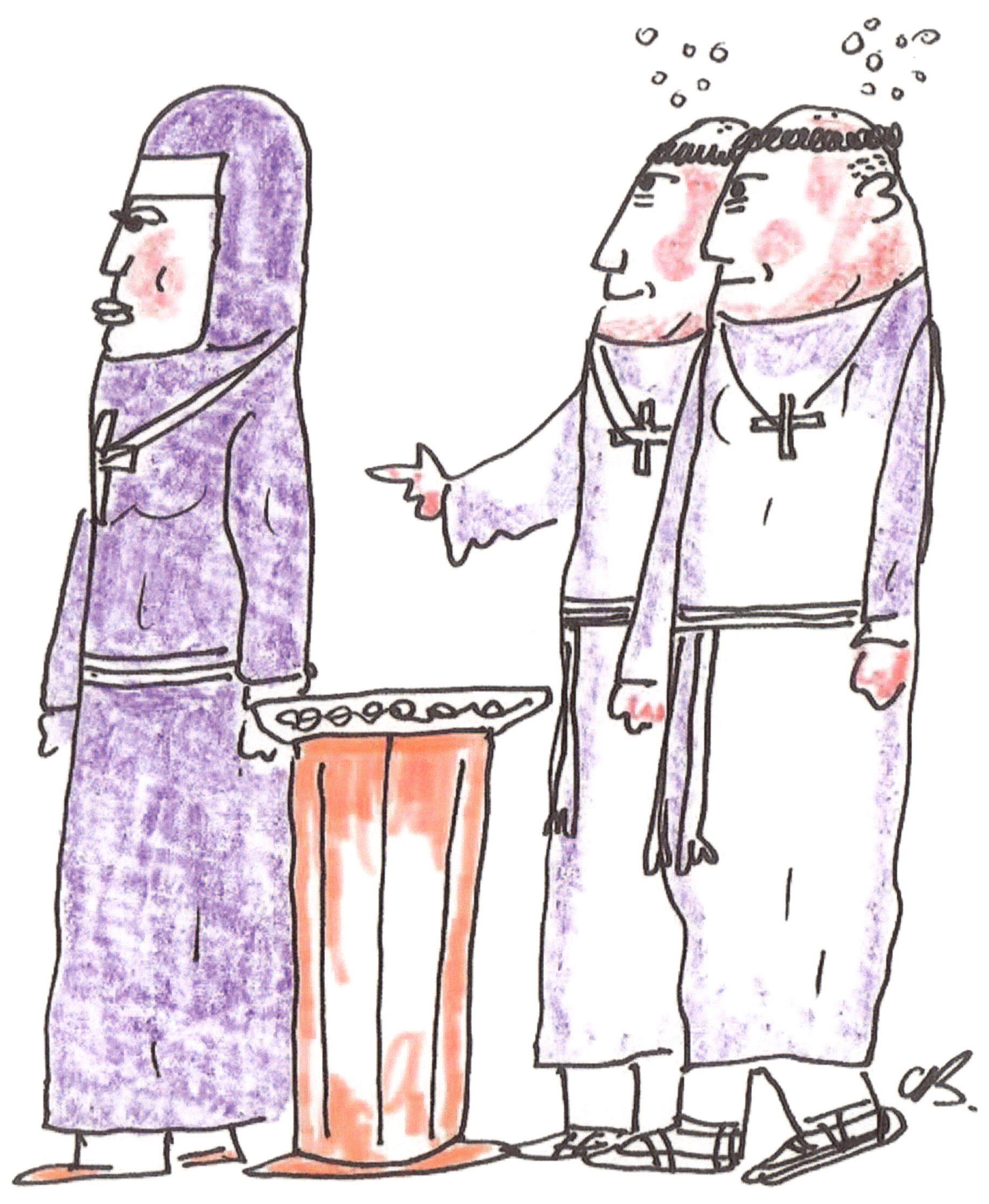

“Now that’s a Superior Mother...
Superior Brother!”

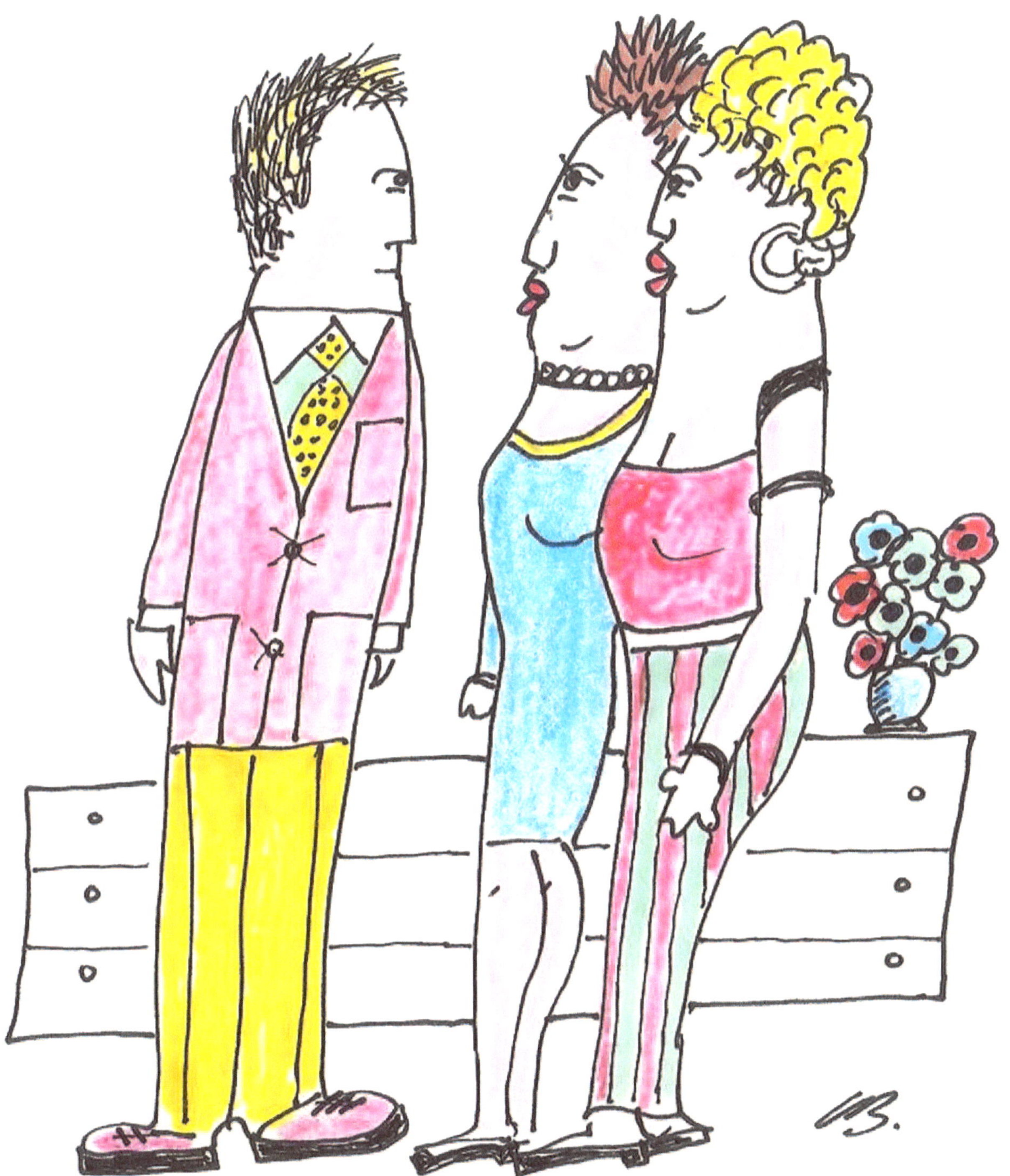

"I hear Joan River's house cost as much as her chin."

www.ingramcontent.com/pod-product-compliance
Lightning Source LLC
LaVergne TN
LVHW070131110826
845147LV00002B/232

* 9 7 8 0 6 1 5 5 6 4 2 1 0 *